The Gypsy Life

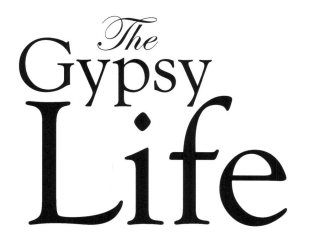

The Gypsy Life

*Adventure in Europe
by Campervan*

Corrie Verbaan

PARTRIDGE
A Penguin Random House Company

To order additional copies of this book, contact
Toll Free 0800 990 914 (South Africa)
+44 20 3014 3997 (outside South Africa)
orders.africa@partridgepublishing.com

www.partridgepublishing.com/africa

For Peggy, travelling the Universe

Table of Contents

INTRODUCTION

In the final "growing-up" years of our children: daughter Melody and son Mark two years her junior, my wife Peggy and I had planned an extensive trip overseas, partly to soften the children's formal education and partly to satisfy a travelling bug that had begun itching when Peggy and I backpacked through Europe for three months in 1973, recorded in "Diary of a Traveler".

By 1981 the itch had become chronic and there was only one remedy. The goal was set in August of 1981 for a trip in March 1983 when it would be spring in the northern hemisphere. This would allow some 18 months for saving and planning.

With Melody and Mark both working it was felt that each should contribute their share, which was estimated at R 10/day for travelling expenses plus airfare and pocket money. I would supply the transport which was envisaged to be a camper van of some sort.

By January 1983 the plan had become: Mark would stay on in Durban and join the party later; a damsel Joanna would accompany Peggy, Melody and me. The finances were now in striking distance of the target.

Excitement mounted as passports and visas were obtained and air tickets purchased. A used camper van was provisionally reserved for us by a Dutch firm in Utrecht. This was going to be a trip on a "shoe string" budget, but we were all determined that whatever shortcomings our limited finances would occasion, the quality of our experiences would not be diminished.

At last the day arrived: 3 March 1983.

(NOTE: Multiply costs in 1983 Rands x 10 for 2014 equivalent. Approximate exchange rate in 2014: R10 = $1).

TO HOLLAND

The whine of the Boeing 747 engines signaled the start of our six month European "safari". Rucksacks, kettle tied on, nestled snugly in the aircraft's hold, while we nestled snugly into our contoured seats to the soporific strains of a symphony squirming out of the speakers. Peggy hates flying. As the plane lumbered to its holding position at the start of the runway, her nails bit deeply into the lush pile of the armrests. When she next became aware of herself, some ten kilometers of empty space extended below our seats and her armrests would require re-upholstering. Despite all assurances to the contrary, Peggy could not believe that a 350 ton metal monster could do what this 350 ton metal monster was manifestly doing, namely, acting like a bird.

Dinnertime provided a distraction. Passengers, with quiet desperation, tugged at diabolical plastic covers through which small heaps of semi-recognizable food portions smugly watched the struggle. After dinner - a movie. There was something decidedly odd about a planeful of people seated in serried ranks watching a small flickering screen in the dead of night, thousands of metres above the Atlantic Ocean in an elongated metallic "cigar" tube.

We made a short refueling stop at a dot in the ocean, Ilha de Sol, where passengers trooped out to wander about an uninspiring airport terminal for twenty minutes before trooping aboard again.

Boring on through the black of night, the compass heading showed our way to our penultimate stopover, Frankfurt-am-Main: the cockpit informing us the estimated time of arrival to be 0800 hours; air temperature 3 deg.C with a slight ground haze. Then, on to Schipol Airport at Amsterdam, where the passenger conveyor made easy work of the few hundred metres from the aircraft to the main hall where we collected our backpacks. These were heaped at the bus stop outside the terminal making it look like a garbage pick-up point.

An hour's ride through flat, misty meadows in a pleasantly warmed bus found us in Utrecht, and shortly thereafter in proud possession of a 1974 VW Kombi. The vehicle had been converted into a campervan and boasted the following mod.cons: facing bench seats with foam cushions and storage space below; a detachable table which, when fitted at seat level, formed a double bed; cupboards had been fitted along one side; a double-burner gas stove provided with 12kg cylinder; a stainless steel sink with drainer and tap which could pump up water from either of two 10 litre canisters below the sink.

The original roof had been removed (it was almost obscene to see it lying there in the workshop, edges jagged as if the dismemberment had been done with a giant can opener). A high level fibre-glass top had been fitted, thereby giving standing headroom inside the camper. This also allowed three boards to be positioned above window level which provided two additional sleeping spaces. With half a metre clearance to the roof, these bunks were to provide us with much entertainment when Melody and Joanna retired at night. After the sleeping bags were laid out, the girls would have to climb up and slide into their bags feet first. Peggy was appointed official "shover up", heaving the two bodies into place like sacks of mealies (maize) onto the top shelf in the pantry. Later as the weather warmed up, the girls were able to use the pup tent which we had brought along as emergency accommodation. The raised roof also provided a large storage area over the cab. A final homely touch was added by curtains at the windows. A track had also been fitted above the windscreen and side windows so that the driver's compartment was included in the general area with curtains drawn.

Formalities for vehicle ownership are simple and effortless in the Netherlands. The transfer is completed at any post office – and that's it! No roadworthiness test, no red tape, and no further charge if the vehicle had already been registered for that year.

In becoming accustomed to driving on the right-hand side of the road, I provided the company with many an exciting moment during lapses of attention when head-on collisions seemed imminent. The weather in the Netherlands at this time, early March, was very different from the weather we had left behind in Durban. Crunchy morning frost was followed by days of cool crispness that called for woolly hats, gloves and scarves.

We spent a night on the marine drive near the motor-racing circuit at Zandvoort. Next morning we were asked to move by a roadside vendor whose "lot" we had inadvertently occupied. He towed his caravan into place, opened up one side, hung out some bunting and advertising and was ready for the day's Hungry. We could not resist for long. I marched over and soon we were enjoying "gebakte mosselen" (fried mussels) for breakfast.

Later, we visited the market place at nearby Haarlem and soon felt the relaxed atmosphere that was to persist through the Netherlands. The people are friendly, the houses quaint, the streets cobbled and the transport two-wheeled. Bicycles seemed to be everywhere: bearing old and young, male and female – sometimes both, and at least one young mother had a child at front and back in neat wire baskets. We were pleasantly astonished by the consideration shown to cyclists by motorists. In fact we were told that the authorities come down heavily on any motorist that has the misfortune of knocking over a cyclist. It was difficult not to compare the average South African driver's almost total lack of consideration for cyclists and motorcyclists. Not to speak of the lesser mortals, pedestrians. (This fact may be "suicidally" confirmed by the reader at his nearest zebra crossing in South Africa).

We came across our first horse-drawn "draai orgel" (barrel organ), just off the market square and this provided the "atmosphere" – its strident notes no longer cranked out by hand, but instead by a small petrol engine – ah, this age of technology!

Following the road northwards, we called in at the very pretty village of Volendam on the south bank of the Ijsselmeer, an enormous inland sea. Here the locals still wear their traditional dress. We bought a selection of cheeses and fresh rolls and parked at the little harbor for lunch. Afterwards: a stroll amongst the houses, sectioned off by a network of canals; rowing boats drawn up on neatly trimmed lawns; roads connected by wooden bridges or the occasional larger draw-bridge; here a pair of swans idling away the afternoon and there a family of ducklings paddling frantically behind mother. With so much water available in the Netherlands in the form of canals, wild ducks and other waterfowl abound. The good natured Dutch frequently erect a woven grass nesting box for birds, in appearance like a large-mouthed vase fastened horizontally to a post in the ground

Our next destination was Friesland in the north, the "rebel" province of the Netherlands. To get there we used the Afsluitdijk (Cut-off dike) the 30 km long double-carriageway dike separating the Waddenzee from the Ijsselmeer. At Leeuwarden, capital of Friesland, we met for the first time my cousin and her husband who offered us their hospitality for a few days. On one occasion we hired bicycles at the railway station and spent the afternoon wobbling precariously through the countryside, a venture considered to be successful by the absence of "roasties" at the day's end. Visiting friends of the family, we were treated to tea and snoeperij (cakes) and thereafter we would refer to treats as "snoep". Later our host showed us the interior of a typical Dutch barn. This housed their bovine population who would remain inside as they had done through the winter, until the weather was warm enough to be released into the meadows. However, they seemed happy enough in their thick rich atmosphere of manure and urine, tails tied daintily to a rope overhead to prevent them from becoming soiled.

An afternoon's excursion found us at the attractive village of Hinderlopen, this time on the northern bank of the Ijsselmeer. Here the inhabitants practice floral painting and few household items escape their art: chairs, cabinets, wardrobes including smaller items such as egg-cups, mugs and bowls, all prettily decorated with floral designs in pastel colours.

A feature of the Dutch life-style seems to be the diminutive scale of objects. From the tiny 10 cent coin (called a dubbeltje) to the typically small house sited on a postage stamp plot and constructed from bricks half the normal size. This contributes to the charm and quaintness of places. Almost as if the Dutch in following this trait aspire to perfection in things diminutive, they have built Madurodam. Near The Hague, it comprises an extensive "mini-town" of outstanding ingenuity. Constructed to "toy soldier" scale, models of famous Dutch buildings, churches and so on are exquisitely detailed. Scenes spring to life (fed by a dubbeltje): a wedding procession with organ music; a fun-fair with carousel and hurdy-gurdy; a military parade to brass band accompaniment; in the docks a fire breaks out on an oil tanker, within seconds a fire-boat directs a jet of water at the blaze.

Of course not everything in this country is diminutive. Take for example the farmhouse/barn. These gigantic structures loom in the distance through the morning mist like a typical Reef mine-dump. Or perhaps like a colossal queen termite, the front end (head) housing the family, dominated by the vast bulk of the integral barn (abdomen) which accommodates the dairy herd and other farmyard creatures through inhospitable winters. An interesting snippet of history pointed out to us by my cousin was the "terps". This is a hillock upon which the important town buildings were located a few hundred years ago, before dykes had been constructed. Once a month at high spring tide, the country folk would repair to the terps to escape the flooding. Towns with names ending in "um": Workum, Dokkum and so on were "terps".

Our track now lay southwards. Stopping at Zwolle to stretch legs we noticed a wedding ceremony about to be conducted in the elegant old town hall. The uniformed attendant was about to close the large doors when he beckoned us to enter. We took our places on a wooden bench and witnessed a charming civil ceremony conducted by a large, kindly looking magistrate wearing a black gown. The bride and groom, both very young, sat facing him with a huge floral bouquet to one side. A small knot of friends completed the scene which was set under the timber beams of the venerable old room, sunlight streaming in through leaded glass windows. The bridegroom was dressed in a trendy, pale suit with bow-tie. She wore a blouse, knickerbockers and moccasins. The magistrate explained their marital obligations in a fatherly way and when it was all over, the usual confetti, a modern day substitute for flower petals, made its appearance and they were driven off in a cute little square-backed vintage car.

Back on the road again, with shadows lengthening, we made for our proposed overnight stop at Arnhem. We arrived at the outskirts as the last light was fading when "BANG", an airborne missile, probably a stone, changed the state of the windscreen from wholeness to fragmentation. This undoubtedly caused in us a shortening of expected lifespan as the glass instantly crazed into opacity. Peering myopically through an un-cracked fragment amid heavy traffic, we limped into the campsite, a magnificent 40 hectare forest. With part of the windscreen missing and sub zero weather outside it was a frigid night in the camper!

A telephone call to the supplier of our camper next morning established that another windscreen could be fitted, but this meant driving the 50 km back to Utrecht. Preparations were made: remove remaining glass fragments; form a partition behind the driver's seat with the foam cushions; and, in my case, don all the warm gear available – two pairs of gloves, three pairs of socks, two trousers, jerseys, jacket, woolen cap and finally a scarf wrapped around my face. Result: the appearance of an obese terrorist setting out on a mission. With wife and girls behind the partition ensconced in blankets, sleeping bags, etc. we set off for Utrecht. An icy blast entered the front window like a solid wave of invisible piranha fish whose needle teeth tore at my clothing in an obsession to reach and freeze the skin beneath. It became necessary to constantly to flex fingers and toes to prevent all sensation from disappearing. At Utrecht a new windscreen was quickly fitted (free of charge), and once more the "safari" was underway.

We returned to Arnhem briefly to visit the Kroller-Muller museum which houses an extensive collection of Vincent van Gogh's works and then headed for the German frontier.

TO GERMANY

There was an excitement about crossing a frontier into a new country which repeated itself each time we crossed a frontier into the eleven countries we visited. This event, sometimes accompanied by frustrating red tape, the cancer of our bureaucratic world, nevertheless always held the promise of new experiences, new customs, money, language and the anticipatory thrill of the unknown, all of which is probably the raison d'etre for travelling. We stopped at the border town of Emmerich where we cashed traveler's cheques and had lunch on the bank of the Rhine River.

We now plunged into the traffic maelstrom which surrounds the industrial area: Duisburg – Essen - Dusseldorf. In these parts the autobahns (motorways) emit a traffic roar 24 hours a day. Here we became hopelessly lost in our search for a campsite. Even with a detailed street map I found it impossible to reach our goal even though I knew exactly where it was – on the map! Eventually we found the campsite having telephoned the camp manager for directions. The following day we called at the Hotel Intercontinental in Dusseldorf where Conrad, an acquaintance of Melody, was employed. They had become friendly on a previous trip of his to Durban and he was unaware of our present visit. The shock Conrad received when called to the foyer literally buckled his knees. There was fortunately an armchair nearby for him to collapse into. That evening Conrad treated us to a stroll along the malls where we enjoyed supper – pizza al fresco – while strolling.

The German young folk appeared to enjoy their revels as nightspots and pubs were thronged. Window-shopping at some of the more elegant Dusseldorfer stores drew gasps from our ladies at the prices: shoes R 250; skirts and blouses R 150 to R 250; perhaps Madame would care for this chic number for a paltry R 500, and what about this fine leather jacket for Herr Dokter, only R 1000? (Multiply by 10). That night we slept at the distinguished Dusseldorf Yacht Club, overlooking the Rhine – in the parking lot!

Other than Switzerland, Germany appeared to be the most affluent country that we visited. Germans are well dressed, drive late model cars and have an unequalled array of goods and foodstuffs to choose from in their many shops and supermarkets. Even as tourists in other countries, Germans were conspicuous by their luxuriously appointed motor-homes and caravans, wind-surfers and speedboats. Someone once truly stated that although Germany had lost the war, she had won the peace – by dint of hard work no doubt. We stumbled on a supermarket chain by the name of ALDI where groceries were extremely cheap, even by South African standards. Prices are kept down by the simple expedient of cutting costs by minimizing staff numbers. There is no attempt at lavish presentation or promotion of items; cartons are stacked, the top one opened and customers simply take what they require. Price labels are not affixed to goods as prices are displayed on boards suspended above the relevant item. Check-out cashiers reveal prodigious memories by ringing up purchases without any apparent reference to a price list. No packer is provided of course as customers pack their own.

This early in the season (March) campsites gave the impression that they were accommodating many campers due to the presence of large numbers of caravans. This was illusory as the popular practice was to leave the caravan in the campsite through the winter months in order to be assured of a place in the sun when summer brought out the camping throngs. In fact many pitches are leased out on a permanent basis, the "tenants" erecting fences and making paved paths, lawn and flower beds.

It may be mentioned here that camping in Europe is very popular, and is consequently well catered for by the availability of well maintained campsites, conveniently located. Facilities are on the whole good and may even be luxurious with heated swimming pools, laundry and ironing facilities, restaurants and supermarkets. On the other hand, the novel toilets in some Mediterranean countries – squat pans – require a positive attitude, in more ways than one. We soon discovered that wet feet could be expected from some of the more vigorous flushing systems. It was often a case of "flush and run"!

One particular camping document that is worth its weight in gold is a Camping Carnet (usually obtainable at a nominal fee from the Automobile Association). As most camp proprietors require some form of security when checking in a traveler, they usually request that a passport is deposited until departure. Now this is a very unhappy state of affairs: to hand over the responsibility for the safety of one's most valuable travel document to a complete stranger, whose office may burn to the ground or be burgled leaving one passport-less, is just too much to accept. In all cases but one, when we left our passports with the camp office for a few hours only, camp managers accepted the carnet in lieu of passport. In addition, carnet holders as affiliated members of Alliance Internationale de Tourisme may receive a discount off the normal tariff, usually 10%.

Cologne was our next destination and we found a good campsite on the outskirts of the city. On checking in we marveled at the lofty morals of the place when reading a notice that stated "only married couples are allowed to camp overnight". We marveled again when, settling up the following day, I happened to glance in at the office and observed a number of immodest "girlie" posters on the walls. During the night we had the delightful pleasure of observing dozens of wild rabbits frolicking on the lawns, having come over from an adjoining wood. Leaving the camper "at home" the next morning we trammed into the city. Super efficient public transport is typical in Germany, and drivers announce the name of stops on an intercom in sonorous monotone. Carriages are clean and schedules punctual.

The City Fathers of most European cities have realized that streets are for people, no less than the motor car. As a result pedestrian precincts have become common and are well used, with a festive atmosphere sometimes prevailing. A visit to Cologne cathedral, as with so many of the magnificent medieval cathedrals which abound in Europe, is a stirring experience: the vast interior spaces moulded into nave, choir and transept; arches trimmed with sculpted filigree; sheltered by vaulted roofs and soaring domes; supported on majestic columns in stiffly disciplined files; the whole illuminated by the charisma of stained glass windows. Our ascent to the tower via a cramped spiral staircase took a novel "turn". Peggy discovered that she became claustrophobic and nauseous in cramped spiral staircases. All this manifested itself as a condition of semi-paralysis somewhere around the 100th step of the 509 step climb. It required calm reassurance, desperate pleading, physical goading and ultimately outright threats of physical violence to enable her to complete the ascent. The suffering endured during the descent must remain untold and a veil discreetly draws over the scene.

The Rhine Valley south to Mainz, 185 km upstream from Cologne, presented its castles in a romantic sequence. We had the opportunity of visiting and being shown over the excellently preserved castle of Marksburg bei Braubach near Koblenz. Fascinating historical objects were on display in the museum: medieval agricultural and kitchen implements; torture devices; stocks for clamping a miscreant's legs, arms and neck; a chastity belt; an ingenious metal contraption having the purpose of silencing a garrulous woman. Our guide forestalled all offers to purchase this item, saying he had offers beyond counting from American husbands (probably his standard joke).

At the small village of Bensdorff, just off the track, we were invited by the Postmaster, after we had enquired about a campsite, to spend the night in a chalet located in a secluded valley used as a scout camping area called Pfadvinderlager (at no charge). Round a blazing fire we celebrated this brief return to "civilization" with a bottle of champagne, courtesy of Hotel Intercontinental (Conrad). We retired to an attic where we found blankets and mattresses. During the night my sleep was disturbed by a sound of scratching coming from below. Shining a torch through a crack in the floor, I spotted a little field mouse investigating our larder. When the scratching ceased I assumed he had feasted sufficiently and had taken his leave. Next morning after our coffee, I sensed a foreign object to be occupying the milk carton. Upon closer examination, the carton was found to contain a bloated, stiffened little corpse. The mouse had taken a nosedive into the milk during the night. The recently consumed coffee suddenly developed a queer aftertaste!

The roads on each side of the Rhine hug the river due to the mountainous nature of the valley sides. This made the drive very scenic: barges passing by flying various national flags; a ruined castle appearing round a corner. At night an illuminated castle, glowing goldenly against the darkened hillside would seem suspended in the sky like an enchanted palace. The Rhine is marked every kilometer of its navigable course by a large board indicating its distance from the source. The number on the last board before spilling into the North Sea reads

"1320" (km). We spent a night on lush grass at a campsite in the village of St. Goarshausen, which featured in the news several months later when the Rhine burst its banks and washed away a number of caravans from this campsite.

Leaving the Rhine at Mainz we spent a most pleasant day at the old medieval university town of Heidelberg. Having explored the vast fortress which towers above the Neckar River, we strolled through the "altstadt" (old town) where shoppers thronged the malls and students acted a play on an open-air platform. Turning eastward our journey continued along the beautiful Neckar valley into the Black Forest region where we found a good site at Schellbron, off the Nagoldtal. (Suffix "tal" means "valley", as in Neandertal, the Neander Valley, home of our ancient relatives). At the camp restaurant we were treated to a few glasses of schnapps, an aromatic German spirit, by the owner who in welcoming us was probably welcoming the start of the tourist season. From here we took a long ramble through the indigenous firs and pines that go to making the Forest called Black, so named possibly as a result of the dark appearance of the thickly afforested rolling hills stretching to the horizon.

The following night we camped on the bank of the Nagold River at Bad Liebenzell. Snow had been lightly falling during the night and in the grey light of morning, a deep hush lay over the village. Tiny, feathery flakes filled every quarter of the sky, settling gently to earth as new flakes took their places. Peggy, head out of the window, screamed "It's snowin...n...n...g...g!", thereby waking Melody who took up the refrain "Its REAL snow! Its REAL snow! as she gazed at the white surroundings. Coming from Durban, there was much excitement while tramping around aimlessly in the snow, throwing an odd snowball and generally becoming acquainted with the "white stuff", as snow would be called for the rest of the trip. Later Melody and Joanna went ice skating at Bad Liebenzell, a nearby rink, roofed but open sided, and the ice had no inclination to melt!

Snow now blanketed the region and we chose to drive to Baden Baden along narrow back roads ribboning through the white, crispy woods with occasional majestic vistas over the forest. A deep silence lay over the land wherever we stopped to enjoy the view. Those hotels in Baden Baden which share the thermal springs that have rejuvenated the aged and infirm since Roman times, present uniformly austere facades – the very architecture seems to sneer superciliously.

Passersby were also uniformly elegant, as if they had been magically brought to life off the pages of fashion magazines. Turning our backs on this snobbish atmosphere, we meandered along the Schwarzwaldhochstrasse (Black Forest High Street). We stopped to stretch our legs at the Berg Hotel Mummelsee where the thermometer on the wall outside told us that it was 0 deg C; and as if to confirm this, a small lake next to the hotel was solidly frozen over.

This was cuckoo clock country. The local craftsmen produce these clocks in an astonishing range of sizes and carvings. It is an odd sensation to be standing, listening, in a cuckoo clock showroom where the ticking clocks all brazenly proclaim a different time of day and drive the point home with hyperactive wooden cuckoos trying to out-cuckoo each other. One clock, claimed to be the largest working cuckoo clock in the world, occupies the entire side wall of a clock factory. Regularly on the strike, a life sized lady and man dressed in traditional black forest garb, stroll casually out of two openings in the wall above the clock face as if to say "what is all the fuss about?"

Driving on through beautiful scenery and "Hansel and Gretel" style villages we arrived at the resort town of Titisee where before long it began snowing. For the next three days our party would be "snowed in" as snowflakes gently blessed the countryside. The temperature dropped to 2 or 3 degrees C below zero at night and in the morning there would be ice in the sink; the drops of condensation which had formed inside the roof from the previous evening's cooking froze overnight into icicles; the door handles were inoperable from the outside until well into the day. I only discovered much later that one can buy anti-freeze sprays for such things as frozen door locks. We were obliged to walk the two kilometers to the town to equip ourselves with galoshes. These allowed us to explore the area and hike through the forest to the neighbouring village of Hinterzarten.

One of the outstanding features of scenic areas in Europe is the provision of hiking trails, well sign posted and blazed, with distances shown in kilometers and often in "walking time". These trails are very popular and we never ceased to be surprised at the advanced age of the good Teutonic locals briskly striding along the pathways.

Walking on fresh snow (a novelty for us) produces a distinctive and pleasing sound to the ear — very like the crisp crunch made when fresh lettuce leaves are broken away from the heart. There is something childishly satisfying in marching across a virgin snow field and leaving your tracks in the snow. Perhaps fulfilling the same desire a child has to scribble on a white wall; or perhaps a subtle satisfaction derived from seeing a tangible imprint one leaves on this planet, for a short while anyway. On our stroll to Hinterzarten, the crispness of the air matched the crispness underfoot. The branches of trees and bushes drooped under a layer of snow, smooth on top and thickly rounded at the edges: yank a twig on a branch and a cascade of powdery snow tumbles to the ground, and the branch swings thankfully back upwards. On another occasion we noticed that trees glistened in quite a different way. On closer inspection we discovered that they were sheathed in a thin layer of ice. Another phenomenon new to we sub-tropical Durbanites was the occurrence of raining "ice balls", not unlike hail as it is commonly known but with this difference: the perfectly rounded pin-head size balls of ice simply floated to the ground.

In order to warm up the camper, we had previously purchased two small earthenware flower pots which, when placed inverted over a low gas flame, radiated warmth in a most effective manner. The heated pots served at bed-time as "hot water bottles" in the bottom end of the sleeping bags. Clothes washing at our Titisee campsite provided a laugh when a batch of Joanna's odds and ends emerged from the washing machine a uniform shade of pink as a result of a red tee-shirt that was not as colour fast as she had thought. The same machine returned Peggy's knitted long-johns with a gaping hole in their bottom and half the right foot missing – no doubt due to a voracious appetite after the machine's winter hibernation.

One of the less appealing chores was the matter of showering, although a hot shower before bed did serve to warm up the body. However it meant a late trek to the ablution block, fortunately heated, and a contest with the hot shower apparatus. These coin or camp-token operated devices provided hot water (sometimes) for between 1 and 3 minutes. The persistent horror, unless one had a spare coin/token, was that the hot water stream would stop at the point where one's body had been soaped up – leaving the rinse to be done in cold water. A method of washing oneself evolved whereby a small section of body was soaped and rinsed before moving on to the next section. At this particular campsite, Titisee, one freezing evening, I had the traumatic experience of undressing, leaning into the shower cubicle to insert a coin, throwing open the hot water tap and receiving a full frontal jet of ice cold water. I had not noticed the shower rose pointing in my direction as I stood back to test the stream. Thereafter all hot water systems were treated with the gravest suspicion. It was here that the camp management had optimistically erected a notice in the toilet block: "It is allowed to use the brush".

During a period of fairly heavy snowfall, we took a walk to the farmyard belonging to the camp proprietor. He lived in a large timber dwelling that was magnificently ornamented with carvings on the balusters, walls and fascias. Taking shelter from the snow in a lean-to shed, we were amazed to observe several ducks almost completely buried in the snow, and others walking about quite oblivious of the weather. Walking was something of an ordeal for the ducks as with each step their feet would sink into the snow until their fat feathery bottoms came to rest on the surface. On the fourth morning we were able to leave the campsite, but it required the camp tractor, wearing tyre chains, to hitch up behind us so that we could descend, by sliding, the fairly steep iced-up slope to the road below.

Palm Sunday (March 27), and the first official day of summer had arrived. Our next destination was Freiburg, a delightful town that emanated a friendly atmosphere. There were a few awkward moments shortly after arriving, as seeking a parking spot, I decided to use the parking garage advertised by a sign on the roadside. We turned onto a ramp which led us across the main road via a narrow double-lane bridge. As we halted at the ticket dispenser I heard a faint scraping sound on the roof. Peering out of the window I saw that we had struck a suspended height restriction sign which informed us: "Maximum height 2,1 metres". I had forgotten that our height was 2,4 metres and heaved a sigh of relief at the close call of almost having removed our roof. Now began the ordeal of backing up and turning on the bridge, the lanes of which were separated by a kerb. Of course by this time there were perhaps half a dozen cars behind us, more driving up all the time. Trying the spectators' patience, we see-sawed the camper across the kerb in a 10 point turn into the out-going lane. Studiously avoiding the eyes of the waiting motorists, I could nonetheless sense their indulgent head-shaking at this poor Dutch fool. (Whenever I did anything silly in the camper, I took refuge in the fact that the vehicle was displaying Netherlands registration thereby taking illogical comfort in the thought that we were not that which we appeared to be – somehow I feel that I owe the Dutch motoring public several apologies). However all the foregoing would have been avoided had the garage proprietor placed the height restriction at the main road entrance. (Thinks: "I wonder if they did have one?").

Later we visited the lovely cathedral from the tower of which we had a tantalizing glimpse of the Alps. At the outskirt of the town were a number of small garden allotments. Wandering amongst them we mused on the wonderful concept that they represented. In many German and other European towns and cities urban dwellers maintain their links with the soil by means of an allotment such as these. Allotments are formed by sub-dividing a piece of land into small fenced plots, perhaps 5 x 10 metres in extent. To these small havens the owners would repair at the onset of spring. We saw many well tended vegetable and flower beds and occasionally a decorated green-house or tool shed. It is an opportunity for city folk for whom the face of the earth is ordinarily masked by asphalt or concrete, to satisfy their natural empathy with growing things through gardening.

It was now time to say "auf wiedersehen" to the Black Forest and the "white stuff" and head east. Staying on the back roads in order to experience the flavor of small villages, we passed through Kissing, Planegg, Aarch, Au, Aha and Oy, all quietly soaking up the spring sunshine and leaving the world to get on with its business. It was agreed we should make a detour into Switzerland at Schaffhausen to view the Rhine Falls. Although not impressive regarding height, we admired the rugged grandeur of the river thrashing its course over and around giant boulders in a flurry of froth. Intending to spend the night at Oberstaufen, which our campsite directory placed near the northern end of Lake Konstanz (also known as the Bodensee), we were baffled by its failure to materialize where the map showed it to be. As dusk drew on it became necessary to call in local expertise as we preferred to always find a site before nightfall. So, with two helpful Germans poring over maps of the region at a filling station, our destination was located at the southern end of the lake, about 100 km further on. Fortunately there was an alternative site nearby – we'd learnt our lesson of not placing total faith in the accuracy of campsite directories.

The following day we caught the ferry at Meersburg for the short hop across the lake to the city of Konstanz. On disembarking and thinking it to be Switzerland, I showed my geographical ignorance by asking a waiting bus driver whether he accepted German currency. The driver answered "Of course, this is Germany isn't it?" The Swiss frontier lay a few kilometers distant. We found the German sector of the city of Konstanz somewhat different from what we had hitherto seen in German cities. Although the border passes through the city, we did not visit the Swiss side. However we found the atmosphere decidedly lethargic; the pavements shabby; and a noticeable number of down-at-heel drifters, as if these types had gravitated to a city also past its prime. Lack of time did not permit us to stay longer to test the accuracy of our first impressions, so back we ferried to continue along the scenic lakeside route.

We next made camp at the hill village of Wiederhofen which lay above the snow line and pleased we were to be back in the "white stuff". Camp facilities were housed in a timber lodge which looked very pretty set among snow clad firs next to a stream. That evening the camp frau laid a roaring fire for us in the restaurant, the only guests. We treated ourselves to beer shandies, chocolates and a convivial game of cards in ethnically decorated surroundings: wood carvings of hunting scenes; horse brasses and hunting horns; the rich timber wall and ceiling paneling glowing warmly in the fire light while outside a biting wind whipped across the snow lying palely under the moon. Next morning we strolled across to an adjoining ski lift and a suicidal-looking ski jump, where the late snows allowed ski-ers to extend their winter sport into spring. The gable of the ski lift station sported ornamentation of shattered and splintered skis fixed, trophy like, to the wall. The sombre associations of the certain suffering experienced by the victims of Lack of Skill that the broken skis represented, were quickly dispelled from the ladies' minds as the local ski instructors hove into sight. One particular light-bearded fellow with clear, piercing blue eyes and casual mien could have represented the popular image of the idealized ski instructor.

Tearing wife and girls away from Wiederhofen, we moved on to Fussen "Feet", the town emblem being similar to the Isle of Man symbol, portraying three legs in profile with bended knees radiating from the centre giving the impression of perpetual running (would make a good joggers' badge). Fussen is in Bavaria and is the location of 19th century King Ludwig's castle known as Schloss Neuschwanstein, pink, turreted and wildy romantic, and the model for Disneyland. Story has it that towards the end of the century, King L almost bankrupted Bavaria in a lavish spate of castle building. He was not an able administrator and ended his days by drowning in an alpine lake. Views from the environs of Neuschwanstein are magnificent: gorges, tumbling waterfalls, dense forests.

Standard dress for both men and women in these parts are knickerbocker trousers tied snugly just under the knee with long woolen, often colourful, stockings disappearing into sturdy walking boots; a jacket with high collar and topped with the characteristic perky little alpine hat, proudly decorated with club badges and feathers. The second most important hiking implement, after boots, is much in evidence. This is, of course, the walking stick trimmed with silver ornamentation and further embellished with badges a'la hat. Traditional lederhausen (leather trousers) are also in vogue. The German male in these parts is, typically, a confident extrovert, even jolly, and often revealing in his waistline a fondness for the regional beverage (beer) and hearty dining.

We took the north bound Romantic Route, so called because of the medieval villages to be discovered en route. Particularly noteworthy was the town of Landsberg, its archway giving the year 1160. At Munchen (Munich) we located an excellent campsite adjoining the city zoo. It was quite extraordinary to hear the roaring of lions at night – we could have been in the Kruger National Park! On a visit to the zoo we found that the enclosures for the larger carnivores, herbivores and primates were designed to replicate their natural habitat as far as possible. In a large children's, section, numbers of friendly goats roamed unattended and children may feed these and other animals by purchasing a handful of the appropriate pellets from automatic vending machines. You do not have the correct coin? – Teutonic thoroughness ensures you will find a machine dispensing change nearby.

The German museum provided more attractions than we had days to spend. This remarkable institution contains displays to cater for all tastes. Although we devoted a whole day to exploring the museum, many departments remained unseen. Those museum directors responsible for presenting mankind's artifacts to the nation have in enlightened countries realized that the old image of the dry, dusty and dull museum had to change. The German Museum is of this revitalized sort (the Science Museum in London is another) and instead of static displays in gloomy rows of undusted cabinets, there is now a "hands-on" concept whereby visitors may operate devices which illustrate, in a simple manner, the underlying principles. The result: literally hundreds of people queuing for entry at opening time.

Good Friday, and 27 days after leaving Durban. This was the first of two Easters that we celebrated. (The second would be the Orthodox version in Greece, in early May). Peggy decorated a budding branch with nine tiny chocolate eggs wrapped in bright foil, and this made a cheery mobile in the van. Easter decorations in confectionery shops were luxurious to say the least. Rabbits, hens, eggs and other fertility symbols of all shapes and sizes were artfully formed out of chocolate, marzipan, glace' fruits and other toothsome delights too numerous to mention. Behind the campsite was a small Christian shrine, dated 1866, hewn into a rock face and had been liberally garlanded with candles and small bouquets for the occasion. Next morning we joined a large throng in the main square facing the cathedral. We learnt that this was a daily occurrence to enjoy a performance of the "glockenspiel" in the bell tower. This 10 minute scenario features mechanical soldiers, courtiers, jesters and jousters, promenading and pirouetting to the accompaniment of musical bells. The finale is announced by a golden rooster crowing realistically while flapping its metal wings.

Nearby is the Hofbrauhaus where almost a century ago the demagogue Herr Hitler began his ascent to political power. The scene today is a lot more convivial. Hundreds of people, smiling and talking animatedly, fill the wooden benches on each side of long tables. Grey cigarette smoke mingles with the warmth of the crowd.. The hubbub of many voices is obliterated as the Bavarian Brass Band strikes up its next number sending a wash of sound across the hall, and before long many throats will be singing "ein prosit…ein prosit…" and the rows of patrons facing each other across the tables will link arms and sway in opposite directions in time to the music. Lucky to find seats, albeit behind the band, we leisurely surveyed the scene – speech being difficult. We were honoured by the presence of the rosy-cheeked drummer in traditional costume, complete with lederhausen and foul smelling pipe, who sat at our table during breaks. We all smiled affably at one another generating much bonhomie. Tucking into our eisbein and sauerkraut, we watched goggle-eyed as buxom waitresses passed by carrying fistfuls of one litre beer tankards – the only size available.

Life has not always been so merry as we discovered when we drove the 15 km to the neighbouring town of Dachau. The weather suited the occasion with a biting wind and intermittent drizzle from a dull, leaden sky. Dachau is better known as a World War 2 concentration camp than as a town. This has inspired the Dachau Town Council to issue a leaflet explaining that although the name of Dachau carries the unfortunate association of the camp, tourists are urged to visit and appreciate the town itself: the medieval palace, old quarter, and so on. The approach to the camp is forbidding enough with stark watch towers regularly spaced along a barbed wire fence. An inner fence created a 3 metre wide "no man's land", entry into which by prisoners resulted in being fired upon from a watch tower without warning.

There is only one entrance to the camp and the inscription wrought into the iron-work of the gate reads "ARBEIT MACH FREI" (Labour Liberates), the dictum that held true for over thirty thousand poor wretches whose souls were liberated from their bodies between the years 1933 and 1945. All the original buildings: administration block, prison and crematorium have been retained in their original condition except the prefabricated prisoners' barracks which were demolished shortly after seizure by the Allied forces. There were originally 34 barrack blocks each designed to accommodate 208 prisoners. As the Third Reich expanded, overcrowding resulted in up to 1600 prisoners having to share each block. One such building has been reconstructed and refurbished, and together with the original buildings form the memorial museum. A large well documented poster display as well as daily film shows of actual documentary footage describe the times and events when the camp was in "business". The avowed purpose of the museum is to keep alive in men's memories the brutality that human beings are capable of. By this means it is hoped that suitable checks and restraints will be provided to prevent a similar slide to barbarism in future. A modern, surrealistic metal sculpture was erected in 1968 overlooking the "appellplatz" (roll-call square) which at a distance looks like scaffold tubing lying in tumbled disarray. Closer inspection reveals an ingenious, and pathetic, portrayal of victims' bodies in the close confines of communal death: stick-like arms, legs with bulging knee joints, skin covered metal skeletons hopelessly intertwined. The scene can be described but not one's feelings.

TO AUSTRIA

We now headed back south along the Alpen Strasse into the Bavarian Alps, every turn of the road revealing a new picture-postcard scene: snowy mountains, pine slopes, streams, waterfalls and lakes. At the Scharnitz Pass we plummeted down the 1 in 6 grade into Austria, and Innsbruck, a city spread languidly in the broad valley between the Bavarian and Tyrolean Alps. Here the glorious unfolding of Spring had brought green lushness to the land and coloured dainties to the window boxes of the gabled wooden houses. Next winter's firewood had already been neatly, even decoratively, stacked under the eaves. An enthusiastic carver had, in his garden, a large tree bole carved and painted to look like a mischievous Spirit of the Woods. We detoured out of the valley to the alpine resort of Kitzbuhl where we camped next to a lake. A stroll of a few kilometers brought us into the village where we came across a politician making a thundering political address by way of a public address system. His voice boomed down the streets while his stern visage stared self-righteously from a poster. The scene was a typical rally with one significant difference – there was no audience present. In fact the street was completely deserted other than ourselves. We felt a little embarrassed on his behalf and we walked by with averted eyes and pretended not to see him. It was perhaps to his credit that the apparent total absence of public interest had not diminished his enthusiasm. On the other hand he may simply have been savouring the sound of his own voice, a trait all too common in public speakers.

A piece of Germany pokes into Austria, like an alpine appendix, and thither were we bound to visit Berchdesgaden. This is a village high in the mountains where Hitler kept his High Command when things were still going well for him. En route we passed through a tiny Austrian village called Lofer where the people seemed very relaxed! Across the frontier we climbed the mountain road to Berchdesgaden, and the scenery was magnificent. In the town we stopped and pondered at a German Wehrmacht (military) cemetery. An elderly lady dressed completely in black, even to the head-scarf, was gently tending one of the graves, and this simple act powerfully symbolized how the ravages of war draw no national or political distinctions when it comes to serving up suffering to the innocent. We had also visited Allied war cemeteries and each time the overriding impression was of the sheer waste of human potential as grave after grave mutely informed that he was 21 years old, he 24, another 18 and so on — the ranks and files of headstones in each cemetery testament to the obtuseness of power politics.

The former German HQ is today an American army base where the focal point is the Hotel General Walker. Here only American currency is used. An extensive underground bunker system, tunneled an average of 30 metres into solid bedrock, comprises about 4400 sq.metres of living spaces, interconnected by 4 km of tunnels. This place, actually Obersalzburg, was Hitler's residential area between the years 1923 and 1945. Shortly after the end of the war, the American authorities deemed it necessary to raze Hitler's house, the "Berghof" where Mussolini, Chamberlain and others met in 1938 as there were indications that the house would become a shrine for those with left-over Nazi sympathies.

We later visited the salt mine in Berchdesgaden where tourists don replica miners' clothing. This comprised baggy cotton trousers with a strap-on leather seat, a loose jacket and a pill-box hat. Thus accoutered we were whisked along at high speed on a miniature train, the open "coach" comprising a long wooden seat which one straddled, cycle fashion, flinching as the tunnel walls whizzed by only centimeters away. The purpose of the leather seat became clear when we were directed to descend some 30 metres on a miner's slide - a highly polished "super-banister" - which provided much mirth to those brave souls who had taken the "plunge" and were now awaiting their fellows' turn to descend. This was followed by an eerie journey by raft across an underground lake; a short film with an unintelligible soundtrack on salt mining techniques; an illuminated display of rock-salt crystals; and finally a hair-raising ride back out to daylight.

Back into Austria – destination Salzburg, (we of course now had first-hand knowledge of why the city was so named – Salt Mountain), built on the site of an ancient Roman settlement Salzburg is beautifully situated on the river Salzach among the wooded hills seen by millions of cinema goers as the backdrop to the film "The Sound of Music". Overlooked by a rather forbidding 11th century fortress, there is nevertheless an atmosphere of lightness and gaiety over the city. Here the musical genius Wolfgang Amadeus Mozart first saw light of day and his family home, occupying the third floor of a five storey building has been converted into a museum and national monument. Inside one sees Wolfgang's crib, his first violin and piano as well as his and his family's musical scores and letters. (His father and sister were also accomplished musicians). A magnificent statue of the maestro in the square pays tribute to his musical legacy.

We were fortunate to be able to view the theatre where the famous Salzburg Marionettes perform – unluckily no performances were scheduled for that week. The medium sized theatre, seating several hundred patrons, has a scaled-down stage and proscenium, and is richly decorated. The marionettes, a number of which were on display in glass cabinets in the foyer, are beautifully proportioned puppets about 60 centimetres tall dressed in the finest operatic fashions in order to perform well known operas.

A deep impression was made on us later that day as we climbed the long incline to reach the fortress. We had stopped for a breather at a spot overlooking the city roof tops with the sun just setting. The beauty of the scene was sublimated as a great number of church bells began tolling. The silvery notes blended harmoniously into an evening concerto, and we could but stand in awe.

Next day an entertainment in a lighter vein: the "water toys" of Schloss Hellbrunn. This 17th century palace set in vast park-like grounds, was built by Marcus Sitticus, a prince/archbishop with a sense of humour. In 1615 he constructed a garden containing secret devices that when inadvertently activated by unwary guests directed jets of water at them. Tourist groups shown through this garden were treated to a practical demonstration of these surprises causing much merriment, not to say dampness. One trick which was mercifully spared our group was operated at an outdoor banqueting table flanked by stone seats. The host seated at the head of the table could cause a strong jet of water to emerge from an opening in each of his guests' seats at an appropriate moment - no doubt to good, if embarrassing, effect. Elsewhere in the gardens are small scale working models of farm and village activities, all ingeniously water operated. A noteworthy chamber had been decorated as a garden and was liberally populated by imitation songbirds. When set in operation, again by water pressure, the birds simultaneously warbled, gurgled and tweeted in a realistic manner. This produced an almost over powering aural effect as the room filled with the sweetly cloying sounds from dozens of liquid throats.

On the road again, now eastwards. We camped for the night on the shore of the Atter See, protected by a laager of mountains, and were treated to a light snowfall the following morning as we left for Vienna. It was to be a long run of about 300 km, twice our average daily distance.

As usual we followed the principle of keeping off the motorways which, although admirable for getting from A to B in the shortest space of time, generally involved high speed, high density traffic with the accompanying driving tension, and provided the least opportunity for seeing the countryside and villages. We made good use of motorways however in the vicinity of the large cities that we did not particularly wish to visit. By entering the motorway before reaching the city it could be bypassed be easily and quickly and so avoid the stress of being caught up in city traffic.

At last: Vienna. The city is surrounded by the fabled Woods and romantic aura of Strauss. A city of rambling, leafy parks; austere, brooding buildings; a Danube not quite as blue as one had expected; an immense fairground with a ferris wheel a staggering 67 metres high (the height of a 20 storey building). Here in Vienna relics abound of the Hapsburg Dynasty – rulers of great swathes of Europe through the ages until deposed in 1914. A number of extravagant palaces: the Imperial Palace, Schonbrunn, Belvedere and Laxenburg are maintained by the State as museums. The palace of Schonbrunn on the city outskirts, so named after the spring discovered nearby (Pure Source) contains 1450 rooms. The royal apartments are on the building's perimeter to benefit from the fenestration while courtiers and servants occupied the interior regions. The walls are riddled with secret passages in order to expedite, or conceal, movement within the palace. The vast grounds of Schonbrunn contain many fountains and sculptures depicting Roman mythology and history. The Hapsburgs, as with so many European rulers down the ages, have revealed their fondness for things classical, either Roman or Greek, and this trend was extended to Schonbrunn resulting in the contrived and elaborately constructed artificial Roman Ruins. Some distance from the palace a huge fountain portrays Neptune in a vigorous tableau complete with Tritons and Naiads (a sign reminds us imperiously "It is not allowed to step on the Neptune fountain"). On the crest of a hill, a gigantic edifice styled "The Gloriette" in honour of king and queen overlooks the grounds and palace complex far below.

There is a touching circle in the municipal cemetery where lie the graves of composers Strauss (father and son), Brahms, Schubert, von Suppe' and Beethoven. Centrally stands a memorial statue to Mozart who was buried in an unmarked pauper's grave in this cemetery. Over and among these stately stones we observed the joyful antics of bright-eyed squirrels. It was hard not to read meaning in this. The immortality of the music created by these great composers was confirmed by the profusion of fresh flowers adorning their graves. Elsewhere in the cemetery I watched, at a discreet distance, the Western Funeral Ritual. A small gathering of black-clad figures, quietly grieving, surrounded the coffin as the last rites were being uttered. Three overalled grave-diggers slouched on their spades a short distance away. Soon the coffin was lowered and the mourners filed past, each tossing a handful of petals into the gaping hole. The last mourner had barely turned away before the grave-diggers moved in and soon the silence was broken by the hard rattle of dry clods striking the coffin lid as the earth was shoveled in. At that moment I had the strange experience of being identified with the lately departed and strongly felt, empathetically, the mortality of the flesh: that the body is little more than a temporary convenience (or perhaps inconvenience?).

Rambling further through the cemetery we came across the grave of the actor Kurt Jurgens and also the mathematician Ohm. There is an enclosure containing the graves of a number of Russian airmen, victims of the last world war. Their simple headstones were emblazoned with the red five-pointed Soviet star (no crosses) and occasionally an enameled portrait of the occupant. Again the feeling – why were these young men from so many different countries, unknown to each other, each skilled in his trade or profession, why were they striving to murder and maim? Young men in the full flower of youth, who in other circumstances would happily share a pint of beer or a game of football. If one looks back down the ages there has not been a century without wars and conflicts and the 20th is obviously no more enlightened in this respect.

After 5 days we left the Austrian capital and headed for Rust, a small lake-side village about 10 km from the Hungarian border. En route we stopped at an ancient Roman limestone quarry. Over huge man-made cliffs and gullies thick with undergrowth there hung an eeriness caused perhaps by the silence of a place which was in its day the scene of much noise and dust and activity of a working quarry. Within sight of the ancient workings, limestone was being quarried by a modern company, lending a sense of continuity to the quarryman's art. A curio shop on the site displayed a range of fossilized shells, bones and sea-creatures which have emerged from the limestone workings.

Rust is a quaint village on the shore of the Neusiedler See which is about 450 sq.km in extent. Much of the shoreline comprises reeds up to 1½ km wide in places. The average depth of the lake is 1 metre. Another attraction at Rust is the storks. These supercilious birds roost on chimney tops of the village houses where thoughtful landlords have provided a small platform above the chimney-pots.

We now turned south west with Venice, Italy our objective. It was an enjoyable drive through the lush, rolling hills of southern Austria. As the camper needed a tune-up we overnighted at the village of Schiefling where we camped "wild" next to a gushing crystal-clear river. It was April 19, seven weeks since leaving Durban.

TO ITALY

A fierce storm welcomed us to Italy which we entered via the Dolomite Mountains. The run down to the sea took us through flat farmland and we occasionally noticed old, deserted, double-storey stone buildings which looked like labourer's barracks, squatting forlornly in the fields.

With nostrils a-twitch for the first scent of salt water, we headed for the nearest point on the coast and had our first sight of the Mediterranean Sea from the peninsular town of Grado. Here the sea is known as the Adriatic. We also had sight of the squat pans mentioned earlier and to which we had perforce, to become accustomed. Nothing conduces more quickly to the adoption of new customs than an absence of alternatives! The next day saw us in Venice.

Venice, the name, evokes an anticipation that is more than fulfilled by Venice, the place. A 5km causeway carries motor and rail traffic to the principal island, Venice, in the island studded Laguna Veneta. This traffic travels no further than the end of the causeway where the visitor seems to move directly into the past by the act of crossing the first canal. All signs of wheeled traffic disappear. Old buildings cracked and faded but utterly charming, prop up each other along the waterways. The entire city is a pedestrian mall. Sights and sounds abound: the arched masonry bridges connecting the many islands that comprise the city; the slapping of water as ferry boats and water taxis chug softly by; the liquid swish of the gondolier's oar as he rhythmically leans into his stroke, propelling and steering in one deft motion; the soul-stirring sight of lamp light reflections shimmering in a million shards across the wavelets at sunset.

Ferries are the form of public transportation and the embarkation and disembarkation of passengers at the frequent "bus stops" is executed with well drilled efficiency. A sign at one of the stops read "Children under a metre high free of charge". Was a tape measure part of the conductor's equipment? (In the Vatican museum, Rome, this concept has been streamlined to "Children under this line free of charge").

For the tourist, a simple "bus" ride is a grand tour in its own right, particularly as several of the outlying islands: Murano, Burano, Lido are on the regular routes. As with many other Italian city-states of medieval times, Venice had her moment of glory as seat of the Venetian Empire and the magnificence of the Doge's palace and St. Mark's cathedral bear adequate testimony to this era. Particularly striking are the larger-than-life four bronze horses of classical Greek origin which adorn the façade of the cathedral. These horses, cast during the time of Alexander the Great, were taken as booty from Constantinople and the poise and grace they portray explains their desirability. There is very little in Venice to remind one of our present "age of the machine" which, in order to bestow technological benefits on mankind, requires the establishment of industrial areas, factories, power stations, road and rail transportation with the inevitable pollution. Such an environment exists indeed a short distance from the mainland, but in Venice itself an "olde worlde" atmosphere prevails. Water vehicles move at a leisurely pace and the absence of conventional city traffic results in a tangibly relaxed feeling – an absence of RUSH! Add to this the impression of floating on a sea, which the profusion of canals suggests, the sight and sound of water never far away. As a climax, see an evening gondola (if you are lucky a flotilla) bearing a small white light on the prow gliding beneath a bridge while the gondolier sings in a rich voice of glories past or romance present – in a word magical!

Of course the mood of Venice, as with anywhere else in the world, must change at different times of the year under various climatic conditions and so evoke a different response in the visitor. The sea, so benign during our stay in Venice, creates much inconvenience when the tide rises that critical height from a level just below the pavings to just above. Dry land disappears as the sea rushes across pavements, scurries up lanes. We had been puzzled by the low benches we had seen stacked in unobtrusive places until it was explained that these provided elevated walkways at times of flooding.

At last it was time to leave Venice for the trek down the east coast of Italy to Brindisi, situated on the "heel" of the "boot" that is Italy.

Here we would take a ferry to Greece. The journey down was easy and relaxing and sandy beaches alternated with rocky coves. At a tiny village located on a promontory which pokes out above the "heel" rather like a "spur", we missed closing time at the bank, but almost as consolation a man appeared at the camper and gave us several sachets of feta (goat's cheese), gratefully accepted. This gift typified the difference between the east and west coasts of Italy. East coast: less populous; relaxed attitude of locals; countryside flat, warm and dry with large olive plantations. West coast: mountainous; up-market resorts: Sorrento, Portofino, hustle and bustle. As for west coast drivers,...... well, more of that later. Approaching Brindisi we noticed many unusual stone dwellings in the fields. They were of dry-stone construction with conical roofs formed by corbelled stonework, arched open doorways and without windows. We could not guess their age so left it as a mystery. The countryside was very pretty, with an occasional red slash of poppies, yellow and white daisies and other wild flowers. Several hillsides, dry and rocky, had written across them the marks of many men's labour in the form of myriads of stone walls laid out in chequer board fashion, almost indistinguishable from virgin rock outcrops after centuries of weathering.

We were the only campers at an attractive site among pine trees near the beach, a short way from Brindisi. There was clearly a fresh water shortage in these parts as non potable water was used for washing. A feature of this campsite which earned it a place in our memory was a neatly lettered weather-beaten sign affixed to an old rusty swing-seat without cushions and on the point of collapse. The sign read "Only authorized personnel are allowed to operate the sofa". From the sofa's condition it indeed appeared as though special training may have been necessary to operate it.

TO GREECE

With the anticipation of standing on the brink of a new phase of our "safari" we arrived in Brindisi to purchase ferry tickets for Greece. Prior to departure we were obliged to report to the passport control office on the 1st floor of a dock-side administration building, and were amused by the following notice on the staircase: "It is strictly forbidden to stop along corridors and on the stairs, to light any portable furnaces and to eat any kind of food. Please use the waiting rooms which are available for this purpose. Please use the apposite containers for the rests". Apart from the fact that one had to stop on the stairs in order to read the sign, our minds boggled at the thought of the scenes which the authorities must have experienced to cause a need for such a sign – portable furnaces indeed! As Melody and Joanna were jotting down this notice on a scrap of paper for our Collection of Unusual Signs, a man passed by on the stairs and remarked to them "You are not allowed to eat chocolate", causing muffled hilarity from the girls.

We drove aboard the ferry at about 5 pm and parked on deck about a metre from the starboard railing. With much excitement we awaited departure at 19:00 hours. At last, ropes were cast off and we watched Brindisi slowly silhouetted by a setting sun as we ghosted eastwards into the night. Our accommodation, we felt, was 5 star as we had full use of the camper from which we had a superb view of the sea. We made ourselves "at home" for the 21 hour journey. Our camp chairs became deck-chairs. We passed the evening in pleasant conversation in the ship's lounge with a Greek couple and a very humerous lady of Argentinian descent by the name of Daisy, returning to Greece, her new home. These gentle folk, speaking good English, helped us compile a list of Greek words and phrases felt to be useful – words for: please, thank you, bread, milk and so on. Daisy advised "You must always bargain with Greeks, and when you say 'Paso cani' (how much?) you must show all your teeth". This was all very well but, as we discovered, if we addressed a foreigner in his own language, we almost always received a full reply in that language, which left us none the wiser – proving the dictum that "a little knowledge is a bad thing". Although locals invariably appreciated the effort made to speak their language, one had to speak it badly enough, supplemented by "sign" language, in order to obtain a simple reply. English notices in Greece, we found, are no less amusing than elsewhere in Europe. Note the sign placed in the ship's toilets concerning flushing "Please push with strong to run plentiful water".

Legend enshrouded Greece!

Rolling on a gentle Ionian swell, the creaming wake sent hissing back to Italy, the first Greek island Levkas appeared to port, floating on a bed of morning mist. Soon afterwards we passed Kefallinia to starboard, and then the home of Ulysses, the island of Ithaca.

Destination Patras: chief port of the Peleponnese, a large southern landmass which was peninsular until severed from the mainland by the awesome Corinthian canal. On arrival, while the crew were tying up at the wharf, Peggy remarked on the number of back-packers and other young travelers slumped on the quayside, apparently about to leave Greece. What she noticed about them was their nut-brown tans and glum expressions. That little tableau would repeat itself five weeks later when we had to sadly tear ourselves away from this enchanting country. A Greek sojourn idyllic enough to come close to aborting the rest of our safari, as the breeze seemed to whisper "stay a little longer...stay a little longer..."

Tennyson could have been referring to Greece in "The Lotos-Eaters":

"There is sweet music here that softer falls
Than petals from blown roses on the grass,
Or night-dews on still waters between walls
Of shadowy granite, in a gleaming pass;

Music that gentlier on the spirit lies,
Than tir'd eyelids upon tir'd eyes;
Music that brings sweet sleep down from the blissful skies.
Here are cool mosses deep,
And through the moss the ivies creep,
And in the stream the long-leaved flowers weep,
And from the craggy ledge the poppy hangs in sleep".

After disembarking and completing customs formalities, we plunged into a city centre frantic with traffic and signs displayed in an unintelligible script. Many Greek characters (the written sort) bear no similarity to our Roman characters. However thanks to the international custom of using Greek symbols in scientific notation, most words were decipherable, if not understandable. The authorities have thoughtfully signposted place name directions in both scripts throughout the country.

It was approaching the peak traffic period in Patras and we were entertained by the very efficient policemen stationed at intersections mounted on low platforms for traffic control. As it is pleasurable to watch any human activity skillfully performed – the pleasure deriving as much from the appreciation of witnessing Skill as by the medium by which it is manifested – so it was with these gentlemen. They augmented their hand signals with frequent and enthusiastic use of whistles, of the sort used by referees at football matches, in order to emphasize an instruction given to a particular driver. Now the density of traffic was such that this whistled emphasis was almost continuous; would have been continuous had it not been for the sheer physical need for inspiration. As there was a series of consecutive traffic intersections, each manned by a whistling policeman, the net effect on the casual observer was as if he was witnessing as event lying somewhere between a highly populated field of crickets at the peak of mating season, and a weird mystical ritual. The whistlers melodically chirped away, singly or in concert, call and response, point and counterpoint. We discovered later that this form of communication is a great favourite with anyone in authority wishing to make a point, especially those good souls who have been entrusted with the care of archeological sites, of which there are a good many in Greece. Woe betide the hapless visitor who does not promptly make his way to the exit on the stroke of closing time, or wanders into a forbidden area; the air is shredded by the almost hysterical shriek of a whistle advertising the visitor's negligence.

Setting off from Patras we followed the coastline in a counter-clockwise direction around the Peloponnese. It is a small point but perhaps one worth mentioning: as with all life's activities there is a qualitative element present which means that there is usually a better way of doing something (fortunate the man who finds the best way in all things) and motor touring is no exception. We found that when the road follows a precipitous coastline, as it often does in the Mediterranean, the view of the coastline below is spectacular. This view is most often visible from one's vehicle provided one is travelling in the lane nearest the coastline, that is, with the coastline on the right-hand side of the direction of travel, and almost never visible from the vehicle if the coastline is on the left-hand side of the direction of travel. This is of course because of the "keep right" rule of the road in European countries. In "keep left" countries the reverse holds true. Of course this benefit only applies if one has a choice of direction as, for instance, on an island when the advantageous direction may be selected.

Alluring Greece!

From rugged cliffs to beaches of soft, white sand in secret coves; a gently lapping sea so clear that the seabed, sometimes of marble or limestone, reflects the light into brilliant azure or turquoise, darkening with depth to the rich royal blue of the middle distance and beyond; the silvery sheen of the sunlit sea that blurs the horizon into the sky; islets off the mainland fringed with crags and foam; lush evergreen forests and rocky, windswept, scrubby hillsides mantled in herbs; olive trees by the hundred thousand and laden citrus orchards; whitewashed villages spill down hillsides stopping only just in time at the edge of a sparkling bay inhabited by colourful fishing boats; from the frenzied roar of heavy traffic in Athens to the rural clip-clop of a donkey bearing an elderly man or woman of the land, a peaked cap on his head, a black shawl on hers, faces radiating serenity by the lines etched by wind and sun - lines of "text" - the story of their lives: hardship accepted with grace and equanimity; pine forests growing up to the sea's edge, trees leaning over the water as if intent on growing in the sea itself; the country air heavy with the fragrance of wild flowers, giving the honey bees much business.

We detoured inland to the village of Olympia, situated in western Peloponnesus. Here we plunged into antiquity strolling imaginatively through the ancient Sanctuary, the Altis, which was the site of the original Olympic Games. This was the site of contests between locals as far back as 1500 BC and in 776 BC the contests, or Games, became Panhellenic. Every four years a sacred truce would be declared among rival, often warring, city-states and athletes bound for Olympia were guaranteed safe passage. Young men trained fervently for this occasion and every athlete had the dream of bringing back to his "polis", or city, high honour as a Victor in one of the contests, symbolized by a trophy of no commercial value whatever, namely a wreath made from a wild olive branch. Women were barred from attending the games on pain of death, and separate games were held for them. The Games were held four-yearly on nearly 300 consecutive occasions over the following 1200 years until banned by the Christian emperor Theodosius I in 393 AD. The Goths destroyed the Sanctuary shortly thereafter.

The Greek concept of pursuing physical excellence lay dormant for another 1500 years until 1896, when a French baron revived the tradition by organizing Games to be held in Athens. It is ironic to observe how today's Olympics have missed the ideal and purpose of the ancients: to declare a truce whereby all differences between participants are suspended, albeit temporarily, for the greater glory of honest competition in the pursuit of perfection. Although the modern Games have forgotten the Sacred Truce, there is nevertheless a stirring ceremony held at Olympia when the Torch is ignited. This is performed by a "priestess" in company with several female attendants, all clad in classical garb, who ignites a special fluid by focusing the sun's rays through a lens. This flame is then used to ignite the Torch proper which is then borne aloft by an athlete and ultimately relayed to the stadium where the Games are to be held to signify their commencement.

At Olympia, the remains of white marble columns of temples and ruins of buildings connected with the needs of athletes and guests, priests and dignitaries, exude a powerful sense of place. It does not require much imagination to see, in the mind's eye, the bustle of the crowds; the pomp of the dedication ceremonies; the sights and sounds of naked, sweating young men engaged in boxing, wrestling, running, the earth baked hard by sun and countless thudding feet; the dignified and moving ceremonies of victors receiving the olive wreath and in turn dedicating this to God in the Temple of Zeus. The first contest was a running race over 192 metres and the original rectangular stadium has been perfectly restored, with its starting and finishing lines grooved into stone, and the water channel around the perimeter with regularly spaced basins to which any of the 45 000 spectators could descend from the stepped seating terraces to quench his thirst. There were two ways in which a participant could have a statue erected in his memory: if he was a Victor, he would be honoured by a statue in the Altis; if he had cheated and this discovered, he would be given a statue near the stadium entrance and a plaque would describe his offence in detail, thereby ensuring eternal dishonor for his contemptible violation of the rules. We visited the on-site museum where many fine examples of Greek sculpture can be appreciated, in particular the statue of Hermes by the classical genius Praxitiles.

It was time to explore further inland into a mountainous region where we discovered the lonely temple of Apollo Epicureus. The inhabitants of 420 BC erected this temple in thanksgiving for having been spared from a cholera epidemic. Due to its remote location, this temple was only re-discovered in the 19th century and is in good condition, with all but a few columns and lintels in their original position. For all the remoteness of the site, there was nevertheless the ubiquitous roadside souvenir vendor from whom I bought a small brass bell. I had duly said "Paso cani?" with a display of teeth that informed him he had to deal with a Tough Bargainer, I was given a small discount (given more out of pity for the poor accent than my intimidation no doubt), For the remainder of the trip the bell dangled from the rear-view mirror to remind us, if we needed reminding, to slow down when the road was bad.

En route to the coast we encountered an extraordinary traveler, in fact a rather unfortunate fellow. We had stopped on the roadside to attend to nature and were on the point of leaving when a dark-skinned French-speaking man on foot accosted us. (We thought he may have been Algerian). He was lost! Now some people may take a wrong turning and feel that they are lost, but this poor chap was Totally Lost. Striking up a conversation with Melody, our French-speaker, it appeared that he thought he was in Italy, and was asking for directions to Germany! His luggage comprised a plastic carrier bag containing two empty bottles. It crossed our minds that the bottles prior to this encounter may have been full, yet he did not seem inebriated. We were somewhat at a loss and waved vaguely towards Yugoslavia and he ambled off in that general direction. Further on a Greek Orthodox priest flagged us down. He was dressed in the black clothing and tall round hat characteristic of his calling; his beard was luxuriant and his graying hair was made up into a "bun" behind his head. We gathered he wanted a lift and for the next few kilometers he sat smiling beatifically. He jumped out athletically at the next village and had disappeared before anyone could say "Greek Orthodox".

We passed through many small villages, the houses all uniformly white-washed with mostly blue, green or yellow painted shutters and front door. Donkeys, chickens and goats were ever-present, and the older male inhabitants invariably occupied the pavement chairs of a tavern regardless of time of day, except during the siesta time between noon and three p.m. These good folk appeared not to partake of refreshment to any extent but made up for that with lively conversation. Many times we witnessed what appeared to be an altercation – raised voices, unsmiling faces, gesticulating arms and animated expressions, only to hear within minutes a great roar of laughter accompanied by back-slapping and the like. We supposed the ladies to be at home and the younger men to be boosting the national GDP in some far off city.

Greeks in general and country-folk in particular we found to be kindly and honest and although curious at times regarding strangers, never rude or hostile. There are many houses in the rural areas in various stages of construction surprisingly of reinforced concrete (until one remembers earthquakes), but seldom did we see Men-at-Work. An attitude seems to exist whereby life is not taken too seriously nor work undertaken too strenuously, after all there is still tomorrow, and today is for enjoying oneself. It was a never ending source of amazement to us to come across abandoned road making plant – bulldozers, graders, concrete mixers – lying on the road sides in various stages of rusting decay (or perhaps, rustic decay?). It was as if they had been left behind after completing a section of road, no longer needed for a while, so…..it may as well stand there as anywhere else, until presumably, forgotten about.

Back at the coast near the southernmost point of the Peloponnese, we visited Pirgos Dirou, where the cliff face is a honeycomb of limestone caves, many at sea level. In one of these watery caves we were poled along in a small skiff through passages and chambers of outstanding magnificence. The route was tastefully illuminated and the pellucid water revealed a coloured pebble floor, or would sometimes reflect the graceful columns where the inexorable desire of stalagmites and stalactites to fuse into unity has been consummated, which columns now appear to support the vault overhead; the shadows around and between grotesque formations caused strange patterns to slither fluidly as the flashlight played across the scene – shadows that seemed alive as they leapt always just out of reach of the arrogant shaft of light; we heard the chattering, slapping echoes gossiping into the dark distance as the boat pushed its wavelets forward; gatherings of gnomes, miniature cathedrals, an elephant's ear, a camel's hump, a spray of ferns – were all imagined into existence as we floated along the silent waterways; occasionally a flash of coloured fire would burst forth as the white light shattered against a prismatic crystal, giving an impression of the jeweled splendor which Poseidon may well expect of his royal residence.

Cutting across a promontory we arrived at the picturesque village of Githion on the Gulf of Lakonia. Here we spent a lazy day on a golden beach in company with the good ship Demetrios, a Greek coaster of some 5000 tons which had been swept aground almost onto the beach. A rope ladder trailed down the ship's side inviting me to explore the vessel. The holds were empty and the cabins wrecked. Doors hung awry and tables had been upended with litter everywhere. I happened to notice that one of the two lifeboats was missing. What appeared to have the makings of a good plot congealed into one when I went forward to find, painted on the fo'csle in large red letters "WIJ WILLEN WEG MET DE BOOT – TOM". (Dutch for "We wish to take the boat – Tom). This explained the empty lifeboat divots but an epidemic of questions sprouted: Who was Tom? Why did Tom find it necessary to paint the message? Had the crew abandoned ship? Mutinied? Who had created the havoc in the interior? Pirates? From the good structural condition of the ship, (superficially anyway), and absence of perilous situation (or so it seemed) it hardly appeared necessary to "take to the boats" or "boat" as the case may be. Another maritime mystery! We baked in the sun and fossicked among the rocks until it was time to walk the kilometer along the beach to the camper. About to leave the beach, I noticed wooden debris poking up out of the sand. A closer examination identified this as the remains of the hull of a small boat – painted in the identical colours of the remaining lifeboat on board the ship!

In Githion we strolled on the small island, today connected to the mainland by a causeway, which had been the point of departure of one of history's more famous abductions which took place in 1180 BC. Paris, a prince of Troy, in order to improve his quality of life and having decided that the wife of Sparta's king Menelaus would achieve this, carried off the beautiful queen Helen home to Troy in Asia Minor. His justification, if he needed one, was that the Greeks held his aunt captive. (A thought: is a native of Asia Minor called an Asian Minor? or a Minor Asian?). Of course Menelaus would not take this lying down so, together with his brother king Agamemnon of Mycenae, "launched a thousand ships" and so commenced the 10 year war with Troy immortalized in Homer's "Iliad". His "Odyssey" is the account of Odysseus's (Ulysses to the Romans) journey home to Ithaca, taking another 10 years over it. It seems that things between Greeks and Asian Minors were never quite the same after the Greeks razed Troy; fortunately Trojan Aeneas escaped to found Rome. Exciting times.

We now headed inland to Helen's place. Sparta today is an unimposing medium-sized provincial town. Very little remains of the ancient city for the reason that very little masonry fortifications or defensive walls were ever erected. Sparta believed that her defense against invaders lay in the valour and preparedness of her militant citizens. Their motto "Our defense lies in the breasts of our soldiers".

A 5 km drive from Sparta brought us to Mystra, an amazing 14th century Byzantine town, built on a hillside. The view from the fortress on the summit over the plain of Lakonia is breathtaking. The town, with many stone houses, palaces and churches still standing, has been deserted for centuries, and at the cost of some heavy breathing due to the steepness of the paths, provided exciting exploring. Many fine frescoes may still be seen in the churches. Stopping to catch my breath I was fascinated to see a short, bow-legged, elderly Greek lady dressed in black literally bounding along the stony path with the sure-footedness of a mountain goat. Her pace did not slacken even when the path steepened and I felt that here was an object lesson in her vigorous manner and obvious fitness. One cannot help feeling that our sedentary Western lifestyle (walking is for the underprivileged – our car is necessary for even the most ludicrously short journeys), this Western lifestyle is preparing one for an old age of immobility and the attendant ailments.

Now on our way to the Gulf of Argolis we were surprised by the huge volume of oncoming traffic. Later we learned that with the onset of the long Easter weekend, practically everyone living in Athens would be returning to his native village. This gave another insight into the Greek way of life. Athens for all her immense sprawl and apparent sophistication was really populated by country folk retaining direct ties to their parental villages scattered across Greece.

At Nauplion we encountered magnificent scenery – gold and russet vegetation against a backdrop of shimmering sea. There was no shortage of campsites in the area and we camped at Assini in an orange grove. Pitches had been laid out between the rows of trees with reed covered frames providing shade. The trees were laden with oranges and the scent of blossoms still lingered, but these oranges, as with those in neighbouring orchards, were crops that had failed! As was explained to us by the camp supervisor, orange producers who harvest their fruit later than their competitors may obtain the advantage of commanding higher prices, but in leaving the fruit on the trees means taking a risk that a late frost will not occur. This is precisely what did happen shortly prior to our arrival and consequently many farmers who had hoped to harvest late had their entire crop ruined. Peggy witnessed a rather poignant little scene as the farmer plucked an orange from a tree and after a few seconds forlornly dropped it to the ground. Our new friend put it succinctly when he told us "The freezer destroyed the oranges". Strangely in appearance the fruit looked normal, the story lay within where the pulp had withered and was almost without juice. For our part however, we persevered in a search for edible fruit and ended up fairly gorged on oranges and mandarins.

There were at this site a number of German campers and the supervisor informed us that Greece was becoming an increasingly popular destination with Europeans in general and Germans in particular, all seeking to avoid the congestion along the south coast of Spain and France. In Greece one may yet leave the beaten tourist track and find that little private cove or beach where it is possible to camp without official harassment, even swim "au natural". The supervisor went on to explain that an influx of Europeans required careful siting: Germans here, Italians there, and so on. We asked him "Where do Greeks go for their holidays?". He stared uncomprehendingly for a moment. "Where is there to go?" he replied with a shrug, palms uplifted, "We have everything here in Greece". We were to encounter this attitude many times before leaving Greece. An attitude, reflected in their actions and habits which signified "We are enjoying life in our own uncomplicated way; no burning ambition to amass wealth (and ulcers); no desire to become enslaved by technology; we recognize human relationships to be above material values and thus enjoy the company of our fellows; we enjoy conversation and love becoming immersed in political discussion in preference to idle chat about the weather; we will give you advice if asked and those of us in authority will direct you for your own benefit without becoming obsessive about it, and will by and large leave you to your own devices – Greek "laissez faire" – within the bounds of law and order.

It seemed that for all the invasions and racial intermingling that has occurred since classical times, things have not changed much since those times: Greek shipping is still a significant factor in world maritime matters; the "stoas" (shopping arcades) are still there although the merchandise is today perhaps more souvenir orientated; the "agoras" (market squares) are still there, and although the seating arrangements in these gathering places is by courtesy of adjoining restaurants, the talk among locals will still be biased towards public affairs.

The Greeks are today enthusiastically religious and the Greek Orthodox Church, or any main-stream religion for that matter, although differing from classical beliefs in certain novel concepts, there is little material change (in broad terms) from classical times in the act called Worship in relation to Zeus (Deus, the father) and the lesser gods and goddesses (His agencies). This direct link may be seen where the so-called pagan temples have been converted to Christian churches. In fact on the island of Thassos (more of which, later) we saw a tiny church building sited within the projecting stone foundations of an ancient temple. Indeed even the Parthenon has seen service as a Christian church and Moslem mosque since the old times. There is a tangible sense of pride of connection enjoyed by modern Greece with the ancient civilization which produced:

Legislators like Solon and Pericles;
Philosophers like Plato and Socrates;
Mathematicians like Pythagoras and Euclid;
Scientists like Aristotle and Hippocrates;
Social commentators like Aesop and Aristophanes;
Historians like Herodotus and Homer;
Architects like Phidias and Polycleitus;
Dramatists like Aeschylus and Sophocles.

All these, and others, have shaped or influenced human development and culture in the western world down to the present time.

En route to the southern tip of this particular promontory in the Peloponnese, we stopped at the ancient sanctuary of Asclepios at the place Epidauros. Asclepios who lived around the 13th century BC was known for his healing powers, symbolized by a serpent. A pair of twining serpents yet adorn the caduceus, a medical insignia. Many centres combining worship and healing, called Asclepia, were established throughout Greece. He was reputed to be the grandfather, 17 times removed, of Hippocrates, the creator of the Oath. The most renowned healing sanctuary was located at Epidauros and functioned for a millennium from about 600 BC to 400 AD. The ruins, amid a pine wood with wild poppies in attendance, are poorly preserved except for the Theatre. Ruined were the Temple of Asclepios and Tholos. The latter was constructed in a series of concentric circles and possibly used for mystical rites (the function of the Tholos has never been accurately ascertained it seems). The ruins also comprise gymnasium, stadium and other buildings associated with the organization and accommodation of pilgrims seeking health and happiness. That the ancients recognized mental health to be no less important than the physical sort, and that the two are inter-related, may be supposed by the presence nearby of a large open-air theatre. Dating from 350 BC the theatre is in good enough condition for the production of plays in summertime. On another occasion we attended a performance of "The Trojan Women", rich in atmosphere but poor, for us, in intelligibility; yet as may have been expected there was much wailing and gnashing of teeth, a universal condition.

Formed in a hillside, the theatre seats about 17 000 persons and is reputed to provide the best acoustics in the world for its type. Such claim may be difficult to prove (or disprove), but the fact remains that the architect Polykleitus created 55 rows of terraced seating in elliptical curves of such perfection that spectators in the furthest row are able to clearly discern normal speech in the orchestra area below, a circular space 20 metres in diameter. Even better, the acoustics are of such renown that tour-group leaders provide impromptu demonstrations for their charges and we settled down on the top tier to witness several of these entertainments in a variety of languages. Typically demonstrated was the clarity of such faint sounds as the dropping of a coin on the sandy ground, the striking of a match, the rustling and tearing of paper and the climax – a deep sigh! Just as we were leaving an American gentleman rendered operatic excerpts in a rich tenor to everyone's pleasant surprise: as a backdrop the valley in the middle distance, the mountains beyond.

It was time to move on back to the coast where we found a delightful site at Kosta, on the beach complete with private cove. That night would see the climax to the week-long Easter festivities being celebrated throughout Greece (May 8), and was our second Easter this year. (We had previously seen Easter celebrated in Munich on April 1). Later that evening, on the recommendation of the camp supervisor (down from Athens for the week-end), we drove the few kilometers to Portoheli where a Mass was to be held. Thousands of people swarmed in the roads leading to the church, situated on a small rise overlooking a charming bay. An impatient firecracker occasionally made itself known. A liturgy was being broadcast from the church and the streets by now swollen with people carrying unlit candles. The hour of midnight was announced by the tolling of church bells whereupon the candles were lighted – beginning at the church, each person lighted his neighbour's candle with his own while conveying good wishes. A tide of light thus radiated from the church until a thousand tiny beacons burned in the night with the same flame. Then began the fireworks!

A fiendish device whirred across the sky at high speed, the banshee wail terminating in a fierce report. Muffled explosions lifted small plumes of water as crackers were tossed into the bay. For all the bombardment, the crowd calmly, almost beatifically, made its way down the hill and generally dispersed. We suspected that the pyrotechnics were the work of the younger element thereby creating a somewhat carnival atmosphere. As the crowd thinned out at the church, we made our way inside to observe proceedings.

There were many icons on display and curiously, a variety of small metal-pressed shapes tacked to a wall panel. The shapes were in the form of body parts: a leg, an arm, a head, which we surmised were tokens of supplication for healing. The service was well attended with many folks staying only a short while before leaving. At the altar a number of men stood facing each other and reading from books, each man in turn chanted in a monotone alternating from one row to the other so producing an interesting effect. The priest occasionally appeared from behind a screen swinging an incense burner and hand bell, and after a few minutes of perambulation disappeared behind the screen again. The church interior was well illuminated by several chandeliers each bearing many candles as well as tiers of lighted candles on the side walls. Amid the general air of sanctity we watched a lad of a more pragmatic persuasion repeatedly sidling into the church to obtain ignition at the nearest candle for his firecrackers. It was 2 a.m. by the time we flopped into our sleeping bags, pleasantly exhausted.

At Kosta we were near the end of the Argoseronic chain of islands and were fortunate to be able to visit three of them: Spetse, Hydra and Poros over the next three days. Next morning we were on a ferry for the short journey to the first, Spetse, also known as "The pine-clad" due to the dense pine forest covering most of the island. Our ferryman had a face the colour and texture of a walnut; eyes that glinted sea and sky; and an expression that showed him to be a man that Loved-his-Work. He suited his role so perfectly by word and action that it would not have been surprising to see him bleed salt-water if he should have cut himself. He operated a fair-sized motor-launch deftly and being single handed was obliged during the trip to remain at the helm. We wondered how he would collect the fares as he had cast off without having first collected them. Greek solution to problem: delegate a passenger to collect the fares. Our skipper seemed to select the youngest person on board, probably presuming that the youngest, being closest to his natural state of innocence, would be the most honest.

A pretty harbor greeted us and after landing we took a long walk along the shore road. The principal form of transport in Spetse is the horse-drawn carriage and the staccato "clip-clop" added a mellow charm to the scene. Houses in the village are typically whitewashed with colourfully painted woodwork. I noticed that in almost every instance where a wall adjacent to the pavement had been whitewashed, a band of whitewash about 15 cm in width had been neatly carried down on the paving at the base of the wall. Although this produced a pleasing overall effect, I could not but read into this a sign of the "Greek system". Anyone who has whitewashed a wall will know that unless one temporarily covers the floor at the base of the work it is virtually impossible not to end up with spots and streaks on the floor where the whitewash drips off the brush. Such stains usually require much effort to be removed. Greek solution to problem: do not worry about spots and drips on the paving – simply paint them into a band as described above. Result: least effort in painting the wall; no clean up of pavement afterwards; pleasing effect.

We arrived back at our campsite at Kosta at about 9 p.m. where Peggy had a little excitement before turning in. The camp ablution block seemed to be a haven for the insect population in the camp grounds, probably attracted by the bright lighting. Moths circled light bulbs while grasshoppers jostled against crickets. Flying ants, when not flying, were dashing about in wash-basins trying to evade predators while occasional frogs passed through enjoying the smorgasbord. Peggy came bounding out of a toilet when she realized she was sharing it with a spider which, to her anxious eye, resembled an emaciated carnivore. A German lady happened to be fighting insects for possession of a wall mirror when Peggy appeared pointing wildly at the toilet and at the same time shouting "spider spider". Noting the non-comprehension on the lady's face, Peggy proceeded to demonstrate the motions of a voracious arachnid by holding up her palm and vigorously contracting and extending her fingers. The lady by this time wore an expression that was a blend of confusion, suspicion and anxiety, and perhaps fearing for her safety, decided that the mirror could wait till morning and beat a hasty retreat out of the washroom.

Next morning we set off intending to visit the next island Hydra, point of departure being Ermione. "Let's take backpacks and sleep over on a beach on Hydra" came the suggestion. It was well received and in a flurry of excitement we packed various essentials, filled a 10 litre water canister, locked the camper and headed for the quay where a ferry would shortly arrive: a crowd of passengers would rush off, to be replaced by a new crowd rushing aboard and the ferry would be off, having spent about 5 minutes at this stop. This time the ferry was a vessel of about 25 metres with upper and lower decks. As the ferry drew closer to Hydra it became obvious that there would be no camping on the beach, at least not on this side of the island. Hydra is a large, peaked mountain dryly poking up out of the sea with nary a trace of sandy beach visible. The absence of beaches on Hydra was confirmed after docking: even the island's drinking-water supply is transported regularly from the mainland. There would be no camping "wild".

Our budget did not permit hotel accommodation so we were obliged to find a cheap room or return to Ermione by a later ferry which would have been something of an anti-climax to our mini-adventure. We were milling about on the quayside at a bit of a loss when a beaming black face appeared, introduced himself as Jimmy and said "You're from South Africa aren't you?" "Yes, how did you know". "I can recognize fellow Africans anywhere" he retorted. "I used to live in Johannesburg myself". It transpired that he was from Ethiopia and was employed on the island. When Jimmy learned of our predicament he directed us to nearby lodgings. This attractive port's houses had been largely constructed by pirate inhabitants over previous centuries. (From some of the prices of tourist wares we inferred that business principles on the island were hereditary). Due to the mountainous nature of the island there are no roads and even the port area is without vehicular traffic. Donkeys and mules provide baggage conveyance and transport to the several monasteries located inland. We followed Jimmy's directions through narrow alleys and found the double-storey house where rooms were let and were greeted by the owner, a tough-talking young American woman. The rent was reasonable although the accommodation was a little on the "public" side. Melody and Joanna occupied a foyer, regularly traversed by other residents, and Peggy and I were given beds in the garden! The head-end of the beds was below an overhang of the house and we spread the tent over the lower half in the unlikely event of rain. The walled garden was filled with flowering shrubs in whitewashed tubs and rose scent filled the air so we were quite happy with the arrangements.

Having settled in, we strolled back to the quay where we again bumped into Jimmy who promptly commandeered a table and chairs at a nearby restaurant, overlooking the bay. Before we knew it there were snacks on the table and wine glasses brimming with Retsina, a Greek wine of resinous character and known for its, shall we say, exuberance on the palate. Jimmy's brother Steve, a quiet young man, joined us and Jimmy entertained the company in a lively manner with outrageous tales of fortunes won and lost in Ethiopia where he claimed to have royal connections. His oft repeated ejaculation made presumably while he awaited fresh inspiration was "Life is sweet my friend, indeed". Three bottles of retsina later (all by courtesy of Jimmy, who produced another bottle every time we made "thanks but we must be getting along now" sounds) the party broke up and we finished the evening with a refreshing stroll along the waterfront and twice around the square. The advertising to be seen outside sea-front restaurants invariably invited one to partake of "FRESH FISHES", or "SQUID AND MANY OTHER ITEMS", or yet again "BREAKFAST AND TOST" (sic). The English predilection for morning toast is becoming an institution. Indeed a dehydrated, sliced loaf of bread is marketed in the shops as "toast", but is little more than bread-slice shaped rusks.

The next day in Ermione after a pleasant ferry-ride back, we collected the camper and set off for the east coast of the Peloponnese. The coastline was, as usual, extremely scenic. As a result we found that we, almost shamefully, were beginning to take it for granted that every new turn in the road would reveal another magnificent vista; with a hint of disappointment at scenery that would be considered outstanding anywhere else. It was as if one built up immunity to scenic wonders if one were so continuously exposed to them. There is possibly a rule in nature that says the greater the contrast between impressions, the greater will be the effect on the perceiver. In any event, we tried to ensure that no beauty was beheld and not appreciated.

At the village of Galates, the island of Poros stood off the mainland by a mere few hundred metres at the closest point. Ocean-going vessels were obliged to navigate with extreme caution when sailing through this strait. We reached the island in a tiny ferry (fare 7 cents each) operated by a crinkled, brown Greek who delegated the task of steering to the passenger seated nearest the tiller (which happened to be yours truly on the return trip), because the piece of string tied to the throttle by which the ferryman regulated the boat's speed was too short to reach the stern were he to steer the vessel as well. Greek solution to problem: the nearest passenger steers.

After a few pleasant hours of exploration, we made our way back to the mainland and continued northwards to the Corinthian canal. When we reached the main route linking the Peloponnese with mainland Greece we received quite a shock. The road leading across the canal bridge and thence to Athens was a solid barrier of bumper to bumper traffic stretching as far as the eye could see and inching along at snail's pace. We had caught the long-weekenders bound for the City and work next day. Corinth was nearby so we decided to camp there and drive to Athens on the morrow. The site was on the beach and we enjoyed a late afternoon swim. Before leaving Corinth next day we visited the extensive ruins of the ancient city where remains of settlement from 1000 BC have been discovered. Corinth was the centre of Greek trade until that function transferred to Athens and its port of Piraeus around the 5th century BC. It appears that Corinth was a city of a thousand carnal delights, supervised by Aphrodite, goddess of beauty and love. It is recorded that courtesans were trained in special schools to bring the sheen of culture and elegance into their profession.

Many Greek cities of antiquity were reduced by foreign invasion, and not the least of these "armies of occupation", were the Romans. It seems however that the Roman conquerors were sufficiently impressed by the cultural life-style of the Greeks to attempt to emulate them. So, as well as shipping Greek amphorae, statues, philosophers and sculptors back to Rome to infuse culture and style into an otherwise prosaic and rough society, the Romans also rebuilt over the ruins of Greek cities leaving many fine examples of constructional craft and particularly, beautiful mosaic floors. Patterns in these floors are generally geometrical although wildlife is often depicted: birds, fish, animals, with remarkable effect achieved by use of brightly coloured glass fragments among the white, terra-cotta and other earthy shades of the fired clay mosaics. We received a distinct impression that modern day Greeks have a tendency to sneer at Roman remains, insofar as remains may be sneered at, and that the preservation of Greek antiquities is given priority. If this impression is correct, it may be partly attributable to that ancient (and un-endearing) Roman practice of carting off magnificent bronze statues to be melted down for use as currency, or weapons to contribute to the further expansion or maintenance of the Empire. Those marble and bronze sculptures that are extant had in many cases been preserved for posterity by the fortuitous sinking of Roman vessels bearing such items and natural cataclysms such as earthquakes or inundations burying those gems under rubble or silt, thereby protecting them from the ravages of time and predations of humans.

At Corinth there were archeological excavations underway and we marveled at the care and patience with which the diggers brushed away the dust of ages past. I happened to overhear a snatch of conversation from an American archeologist walking by in company with a young lady "….and this seems to suggest they may have….". What it was that they may have I will never know, but at this moment I received a tiny insight into the nature of their craft. The excitement (and frustration) of the challenge of fitting together this monumental jig-saw puzzle of some forgotten culture: their lifestyle; implements; levels of skill in art, commerce and science; rituals and beliefs – each new find another microcosmic piece in the puzzle. The aim of the whole: to restore the Past to the Present. We were told that many ancient sites have yet to be fully excavated and that well over 100 undersea locations of ancient shipwrecks have been plotted, awaiting exploration. This information is a closely guarded secret to prevent exploitation by treasure seekers.

Bound for Athens, we stopped to photograph the Corinthian Canal, a gargantuan feat of engineering that severs the Peloponnese from the mainland to allow shipping to pass directly between the Saronic and Corinthian gulfs. As we approached Athens, a very different picture of Greece presented itself. Poppy-flecked hillsides became oil refineries; pine forests became factories; olive plantations became industrial areas. To seaward hundreds of ocean-going vessels were tethered, waiting for……..what?

At last, 2 months and 8 days after leaving Durban, we arrived in Athens, one-time capital of the civilized world. The city was named after Pallas Athena, virgin goddess of wisdom, born from the mind of Zeus. She edged out her Uncle Poseidon, god of the sea, in a contest as to who could provide mankind with the most useful gift. Poseidon confidently produced a horse, but could not match Athena's offering – an olive tree. She thus became the city's tutelary deity and was the inspiration for that architectural masterpiece, the Parthenon. Completed in 432 BC this timeless work of art, along with other fine temples and sanctuaries built from creamy Pentelic marble, is thrust above the city like a royal diadem in a rocky setting: the Acropolis – the marble hues changing from honey to pristine white to pale amber as Helios slides across the sky. The Parthenon contains no horizontal or vertical lines in its construction and the architects compensated for visual distortion by curving the horizontal lines and tilting the columns inward slightly. The gable ends fit the proportions of the "golden rectangle", the sides of which enjoy a unique relationship: the height to the width is as 1 is to 1,618 or as 0,618 is to 1; proportions naturally harmonious to the eye.

Seen from most points of the city, this great rock with its precious cargo is a presence continually felt. The Parthenon, quite apart from being an object of beauty, is a living reminder of the Golden Age of Greece when the human race attained great heights in aesthetic, intellectual and physical development. Even that perfidy of human relations, that odious, social gangrene called slavery – the product of those martial times – was practiced with compassion by the more enlightened Athenians. Slaves were often adopted into the household, even gaining their freedom as did the philosopher/slave Epictetus, who never considered himself enslaved anyway. He only recognized mental bondage as slavery as opposed to the physical sort. One of Epictetus's special quotations was Socrates' utterance at his trial "…my accusers may kill me, but hurt me they cannot".

Our first sight of the Parthenon came as we were entering the city via the main western approach. The road runs in a long, pencil-straight downward gradient and at the point where it snakes out of sight in the distance, a tiny Parthenon seems to float in the sky. Even at that range and amid thundering traffic, the first impression is seared into the mind. We found an excellent campsite in this main road with flowering shrubs and fruit trees, a little restaurant bowered by a lush creeper, unlimited hot water in marble shower stalls (which felt a little funereal) and toilets of the comfortable variety. We would bus to the city for the next few days, and this was an experience in its own right. In fact the experience began on leaving the camp gates. We had to cross the extremely busy double carriageway to the bus stop on the other side of the road. Although there was a zebra crossing painted on the road, it was obviously totally invisible to traffic. We attempted to exercise our pedestrian rights by making a show of striding confidently out into the road – only to be sent scurrying back to the kerb in the wake of compressed air punched out by a thundering 15 tonner. Peggy, bathed in a wave of righteous indignation, proceeded to gesticulate meaningfully at the steady stream of traffic while mouthing her opinion of Greek drivers – but had her wrath instantly undermined by the next truck driver casually blowing her a kiss as he barreled past throwing up a shower of gravel. Any remaining aggression melted away when a dark, middle-aged Greek man in a grey suit approached us and with a flourish, handed Peggy the single red rose he had been carrying. Knowing we had fought and lost, we scampered across to the dividing island and at an opportune lull bolted for the far kerb. It was sad to see the unfortunate effect that this foot-to-the-floor driving attitude had on the canine population, judging by the many corpses we noticed on roadsides. On one occasion, having successfully gained the bus-stop, I was obliged to venture back into the traffic in order to drag a magnificent - but dead - Alsatian dog to the kerb side. Although there is no doubt in my mind that the average Greek is as fond of, and sympathetic towards, his animal pets as anyone anywhere else, we did occasionally notice a casual, almost insensitive, attitude towards animal welfare – in a donkey overloaded or hobbled too tightly, or the young baboon tethered to a pole next to the campsite without shade or water during the day.

The bus rides to town and back gave us a driver's-eye view of Athenian life on wheels, and it seemed a matter of honour for drivers, including our bus driver, to attain the maximum speed possible wherever an unobstructed stretch of road opened up ahead. One late night returning to camp, our driver crossed at least two intersections against red lights and at speeds around 100 km/hour. It was the first time in my driving experience that I obtained a feeling of relief by not looking in the direction of travel. It had become a matter of Faith and Trust. A less suicidal idiosyncrasy of Athenian drivers is the habitual sounding of their horns in short, sharp bursts. These proclamations occur for no apparent reason. Could they be a reflex action in some way linked to operation of the vehicle's controls? Or a coded desire for recognition – here I come, an individual in a city of millions?

It is not only the Parthenon that is of interest to the visitor, we visited: the ancient Greek agora; the later Roman forum in the commercial heart of the city, meeting place for business deals, marketing or simply to catch up on local gossip; the ancient cemetery, where tombstones were carved to depict the departed in a gloriously noble pose; the cell cut into the solid rock of the hillside facing the Parthenon where Socrates chose to drink the ultimate night-cap — draught of hemlock; the remains of the gigantic temple of Olympian Zeus, largest temple ever built in ancient times; we saw from a distance the Greek and Roman theatres at the base of the acropolis; the stadium, built in 330 BC, which was reconstructed to the original design when it became a most fitting venue for the first Olympic Games held in 1896, after a lapse of 1500 years!

No visit to Athens would be complete without spending time in the National Archeological Museum whither most major "finds" are sent. It is awe-inspiring to view the meticulous detail and sheer beauty of ancient jewelry — bangles, brooches, fine chains, amulets, goblets, miniatures; statues and sculptures from the most distant times; pottery of extraordinary grace, decorated with legendary exploits. There is also an impressive collection of gold artifacts and jewelry unearthed in the late 19th century by the German "amateur" archeologist Herr Schliemann, from the royal tombs at Mycenae which had lain there since about 1500 BC. About 14 kg of gold objects (cups, daggers, combs) were recovered including a golden death-mask, supposedly King Agamemnon's, who together with his brother King Menelaus of Sparta were put to some trouble by Queen Helen's abduction (or elopement?). Helen was taken to Troy which ancient city Schliemann is also credited with having re-discovered. King Agamemnon was brutally murdered by his wife and her consort on the same day he arrived back at Mycenae after the Trojan business. If his expression as preserved by the mask is anything to go by he was not happy about it. The fact that he brought back with him Cassandra, daughter of King Priam the defeated Trojan king, as his mistress probably did nothing to help matters.

Two examples of bronze sculptures from the classical era stand out for their perfection. A slightly larger than life Poseidon stands poised with arm drawn back about to hurl a spear or trident, (unfortunately missing), the other arm outstretched in front with fingers sensitively disposed, an expression of Stern

Strength on the bearded features, all resulting in an effect of frozen poetry. The other sculpture is The Jockey by Artemision which portrays a youth of about 14 years as if astride a racehorse. Although the horse was never found, from the boy's crouching posture and determined expression he could have been leading the field in the hippodrome at Olympia. This gem exudes an exciting dynamic vitality.

The Plaka in Athens is the name of the old quarter which sprawls along the base of the acropolis. This area has much character and comprises alley upon alley of pavement vendors displaying a vast range of merchandise: from plastic Taiwanese Parthenons to "genuine" antiques. One tiny basement shop displayed a sign above the stair which led down from the pavement "Please take care of your head". Pretty good advice when you think about it! We treated ourselves to a late dinner at a roof-garden restaurant one evening in the Plaka and greatly enjoyed yoghurt with honey, salad and mousaka, a sweetmeat and a convivial bottle of Greek wine.

It was time to leave Athens and we decided to head south, again following the coastline. An enjoyable drive brought us the starkly dramatic Temple of Poseidon at Cape Sounion. The temple occupies a precipitous position overlooking a magnificent sea-scape. An offshore wind gusted fiercely between the marble columns as if to sweep offerings to the Lord of the Deep. We failed to find Lord Byron's name supposedly cut into the stonework, but we did see a number of names and initials with 19th century dates which had been engraved in a meticulous calligraphic hand. The Kilroy's of yester-century obviously had a style not matched by today's graffiti-mongers with their aerosol paints.

We found a campsite for the night near the Cape which had an odd feature about the ablution block. It was the manner in which it had recently been whitewashed. It looked as though the painter had taken buckets of whitewash and literally thrown the contents at the walls. Whitewash was strewn across the floor, blobbed on the door and spattered across the toilets. We hereafter had a new phrase whenever referring to sloppy or careless paintwork "It looks as if the Sounion Painter has been here". At the same site we had the pleasure of meeting a young man from Pinetown, near Durban.

Pointing the camper northwards we stopped at the simple but moving war memorial at Marathon. A 12 metre high mound of earth covers the ashes of

192 Athenians who fell during the resistance to the Persian invasion of 490 BC. The battle conducted between 10 000 Athenians and an army of 30 000 Persians, also left 6 400 Persians dead. The standard marathon running race, first instituted at the revival of the Olympic Games in 1896, commemorates Pheidippides's 26 miles and 385 yards dash from the battlefield to inform anxious Athens of their victory. It is said that he dropped dead in the agora after imparting the news. It is not surprising that valiant Pheidippides overtaxed himself; he had prior to this "marathon event" run 150 miles to Sparta in an attempt to secure their support against the impending invasion. He was met with excuses that it was not propitious for them just now, thanks, so the Athenians had to go it alone.

After camping wild on a deserted beach at Arkitse, we passed through Thermopylae where the Persian Xerxes was delayed by 300 Spartans defending the pass to Athens. Intent on avenging their humiliating defeat 10 years before at Marathon, Xerxes was shown an alternate route through the mountains to Athens which they razed. The Persians were ultimately defeated at the epic sea battle at Salamis.

Pressing on northwards, we made a minor detour to visit limestone caves high up a hillside near the village of Peania. Relatively recently discovered, we marveled at the silent processes taking place beneath the skin of the earth where the flow of time has all but congealed. At the conclusion of the tour through the labyrinth visitors were treated to a mini "sol et lumiere" performance. In a large cavern, subdued coloured lighting changed position while eerie music filled the air – strange mystical rhythms, rising, falling, so imperceptible at times that one felt to be blending into the dim glow and seemingly infinite void.

Moving on again, we stocked our larder at Larissa, a large town, and soon reached the region of the gods – Mount Olympus. (There is no connection with Olympia, hundreds of kilometers away in the Peloponnese). Basing ourselves at a pretty campsite not far away, we set out next day to explore the mountain. A mountain road, precipitous at times but always very scenic, wound its wooded way up the valley towards Olympus, ending at a height of 1100 metres above sea level. Here we found a timber hut used as a base for mountain climbers and were informed that there was another hut at an elevation of 2100 metres, which traditionally provided bean soup for hikers. Parking the camper and packing a picnic lunch we started out on the footpath without any precise objective other than the prospect of bean soup. The day was warm and sunny, and after walking for about an hour we were surprised, and yet not surprised, when a number of elderly German tourists appeared on the path, striding purposefully in "wandel lust" fashion towards and past us. After lunch, we decided to carry on and make for the upper hut. The beach "slops" worn by the ladies drew interested glances and indulgent smiles from hikers wearing heavy boots as we passed each other. The path climbed much of the way through pine trees in a wonderfully tranquil setting. After a few hours we began to see evidence of snow damage in the ravines where trees lay in heaps like giant fiddlesticks, tangled and splintered. Beginning to feel the pangs of thirst we were overjoyed to find that the path dipped ahead through a shallow ravine and we would be crossing – snow! we had previously noticed the odd gully containing last winter's "white stuff" but they had been inaccessible. We scraped away the dirty surface and brought out handfuls of crystallized snow which were blissfully consumed. An impromptu snow-ball fight, a few "slides" down the slope and we were off again, refreshed but hoping the hut was not much further. An hour later, 4½ hours after setting out, the hut hove into sight. However an amusing drama had to be played out before we could reach our goal. Two pack-mules had wandered down the path from the hut to graze along the narrow track. We had no great desire to squeeze intimately past the beasts and not able to judge the state of spleen of a Greek mule in the shadow of Zeus, decided to make a slight detour up a steep slope above the path. This was accomplished without difficulty except for Peggy who could find no purchase on the stony slope. At this moment the mules began lumbering towards her. She screamed and scrabbled up as far as she could manage clinging to tufts of grass. We were wonderfully entertained at our vantage point up ahead although Peggy failed to see the funny side of it. We reached the hut and gratefully spread out in the sun to recover. The elevation here is 2100 metres, one kilometer above the hut where we had parked. The peak in this range known as Olympus towered a further 817 metres higher (elevation 2917 metres above sea level) presenting a starkly dramatic snow-scape in the clouds. We imagined Zeus and company amusedly looking down at our ant-like grappling in their precincts, especially with that silly footwear. The vegetable soup (not bean) was very welcome. After a brief rest we started the descent and a brisk 2½ hours later were back at the camper feeling we had earned a good night's rest.

Making an early start next morning we stopped briefly at the Lion of Amphipolis. This was the site of an ancient Athenian colony. The Lion is an enormous stone statue sitting upright on its haunches, stiff-backed and proud. 12 metres tall (the height of a 4 storey building) he faces north, the direction of danger for the ancients, symbolizing Eternal Vigilance.

Thessaloniki, second largest city in Greece, was our next stop. We needed to have a bad electrical connection to the starter motor looked at and this was speedily rectified. That night we camped at Agia Triada, a well appointed municipal campsite south of the city, We bumped into a young couple, Ken and Colleen, who had bought a campervan from the same Dutch firm in Utrecht that we had. I identified their camper as we drove into the campsite by the curtaining at the windows – it was identical to ours and the Dutch registration plate seemed to clinch it. More than that, Colleen is a Durban girl and had grown up in the same suburb as had Peggy. They naturally had much to natter about and our paths would cross several times for the following week as we were both heading east. As if the two vans were not to be outdone by their masters' coincidences, Ken's vehicle had a similar starter problem. I recommended the repair shop we had used in Thessaloniki and later learned that Ken had followed my rather vague directions and had the repair carried out.

We now found ourselves in the area known as Chalcidice (pron. Hal-ki-di-ki) which comprises three peninsular prongs thrust out from the mainland into the Aegean Sea like Poseidon's trident. This creates a coastline of coves, beaches and bays to rival in charm and beauty the Peloponnese coastline. The "prongs" are named, from west to east: Kassandra, Sithonia and Agio Oros. The latter peninsula, which we were not allowed visit for the reason given below, has been continuously inhabited by monks since the 10th century who follow the traditions of Byzantine Christianity, also known as Greek Orthodox. At the peak of monastic development 40 000 monks lived in 40 monasteries. Today only 20 monasteries are functioning and monks number about 1700. At the southern tip of the peninsula a mighty mountain rise out of the sea to an altitude of 2033 metres – Mount Athos. We were prevented from visiting this fascinating area by the Byzantine Emperor who, in 1060 AD stipulated three conditions for entry; 1) a permit is required (no problem); 2) overnight stays are forbidden (no problem); 3) women are not admitted (problem), In fact no female of any form: human, animal or otherwise, is permitted entry.

We enjoyed a slow sight-seeing drive along Kassandra's coastal road, rapturous over the kaleidoscope of colours of the sea: pale blues and greens, ultramarine, sapphire and turquoise, the royal blue of deep water. We met up with Ken and Colleen at an out-of-the-way picnic spot (hi, hi) and drove the 20 km to Sithonia and once again, an aesthetic banquet of sea colours. That night we stayed at Vourvourou where we made our acquaintance with the camp hedgehog, spotted by torchlight near the tent. We had strolled down to a rocky bay at sunset where the tranquility was tangible. The pellucid water was undulating gently and throwing off sunset reflections – and a sense of peace.

The next day we could not manage more than 30 kilometres before being pulled off the road at the sight of Platanitsi, a spot where the gentle sea, warm sandy beach, underwater snorkeling, walks in the wooded countryside and balmy evenings would entrap us for the next three days. It occurred to me that if the Greek general Odysseus came across idyllic retreats such as these, with the odd siren thrown in, on the journey home after the fracas with the Trojans, it may account for him taking 10 years to return to his island-home, Ithaca.

During a walk in the countryside on one occasion we noticed a small incident which illustrated the superior intelligence of goats over sheep. A shepherd was driving his flock along a dusty road which forded a shallow stream. Accompanying the flock was a solitary goat. When the sheep arrived at the crossing the leader plunged straight into the ankle-deep stream and the flock followed unthinkingly. However when the goat came to the water's edge he stopped, glanced first downstream, then upstream, before trotting a few metres upstream where a number of large stepping-stones made a "path" across the stream, and so crossed without getting his feet wet. Although this was a trivial incident, the goat acted with a conscious deliberation quite absent in the sheep. On our stroll back to the campsite we were startled by a donkey bursting out of the undergrowth. He raised his top lip at Peggy in a disarming smile of great yellow teeth (was he apologizing for his cousins on Mount Olympus?) and followed us most of the way back to camp.

We did our shopping for groceries and fresh bread (delicious) at the nearby sea-side village of Sarti which had old, charming, vine-laced houses with blue shutters, sandy roads and the ubiquitous square with men folk in eternal conversation. The restaurant sported a sign which read "Sarti by Night" and suggested "high jinks" in the season, it was now May, pre-season, and Sarti was yet Quiet by Night. Our camp supervisor at Platanitsi, an enthusiastic young man by name Stratos, visited us frequently in order to, as he put it, "… to practice my English". Stratos had the idea that he needed to attract holiday-makers to his campsite and in order to provide an attraction (what was wrong with the natural splendor of the place?) he suggested the outrageous proposition of painting giant Walt Disney characters on the boulders along the beach. We were so horrified at this notion that we were bereft of speech. One can hardly imagine anything less in keeping with the environment or more outrageous than coming around a corner in this paradise to be confronted by a 2 metre high Mickey Mouse painted on a rock

Finally it was time to leave. We were still heading eastwards along the coast and stopped at a small village where Aristotle the scientist/philosopher of ancient times was born. This event has been commemorated by a marble statue set in a lovely rose garden. This great thinker set the pattern of the western world's enquiry into the secrets of nature and is reputed to have said "Man, by nature, desires to know" thus directing the search outwards into the universe. This is not quite what the master, Socrates, preached however. Paraphrasing Aristotle's quotation, Socrates might have said "Man, by nature, knows", thus turning the search inwards, instead of outwards, for the revelation of Knowledge. It is interesting to speculate that had the spirit of Socrates been followed rather than Aristotle's, people of our planet today may have shown greater wisdom and harmonious co-existence than technological achievement.

The road carried us through scrubby countryside, the weather warm and dry. This was tortoise territory and we stopped whenever we saw one crossing, or about to cross, the road. Crossing at one kilometre per hour would surely reduce its life expectancy to a few minutes (evidence of tortoise "road-kill" confirmed this notion). Peggy would leap out, pick up the tortoise, carry it off into the bushes and set it down facing away from the road, hoping he would accept the new heading.

At our next campsite in Kavala, an attractive port, we found a pitch next to…yes, Ken and Colleen. We celebrated the reunion over a bottle of Domesticos (marginally less harsh than Retsina). Their intention of taking the ferry across to the nearby island of Thasos coincided with ours and so we agreed to travel together. But first, make a visit to the town. Kavala is a picturesque fishing port where the wharf was thickly spread with fishing nets, tended by grizzled fishermen, while their steeds of the sea were tethered nearby on a barely noticeable swell. We climbed cobbled alleys to the 13th century Venetian fortress where the wind sighed through the battlements; the Aegean shimmered; and Thasos, almost concealed by haze sent out her siren's song. Descending from the fortress we were just in time to visit Mohamed Ali's magnificent house, now a museum, which was about to be closed for the day. This elevated timber dwelling with shaded verandahs and shuttered windows overlooked the bay. It belonged to the militant Islamic leader who founded the ruling dynasty in Egypt in the 18th century. This rule terminated in the 1950's when king Farouk, a descendant of Ali, was deposed. There is a magnificent bronze statue of Mohamed Ali in the courtyard portraying the character of Warrior and Conqueror – straight backed and be-turbanned, stern of visage and brandishing a scimitar; his horse, nostrils flaring, in a posture of power controlled.

Today – Thasos. By mid morning Ken and I had driven the campers aboard the ferry. As the vessel drew away from the mainland we again sensed the excitement and anticipation of heading into the unknown. Thasos would be the last Greek island we were able to visit on this trip – the lure of the legendary islands in the Cyclades and Dodecanese groups, Crete and Rhodes, will no doubt one day get the better of us – but for this trip, Thasos was to be five days of peaceful perambulation (anti-clockwise) round the coast.

Thasos had been known from antiquity as "The jewel of the Aegean" as well as "The blessed isle". It is not difficult to see why. Some thirty kilometers in diameter the island boasts forested mountain slopes, plains flourishing with olive plantations, pine trees along a coastline interrupted by sandy coves, and a marble sea bed reflecting the sun through the translucent clarity of the water. Passing through a wood I did a "double-take" at what appeared to be litter strewn about. As this would have been totally unbelievable I investigated further – only to find that what appeared to be litter was, in fact, scattered lumps of fragmented marble!

Our first sunset on the island could have come straight out of a Hollywood film extravaganza. The sun cast a vibrant golden path on the still water as it disappeared slowly below the horizon as we watched enchanted from the small harbor at Limenas. Enjoying this twilight transition, an offshore zephyr arose and drifted thousands of velvety puffballs from nearby trees across the quayside. The sky seemed to be filled with blossoms, or snow flakes (without the cold) gently settling on the ground and water's surface, lacking only a celestial choir to complete the scene.

For almost a week we snorkeled, sunbathed, swam and collected marble pebbles, with occasional drives into the interior to villages that have probably not changed much over the last hundred years. At one village, Theologos (pop.1132), we were invited by a Greek lady to partake of the fruit of her mulberry trees, several of which bore plump white berries, with a subtly sweet taste. The husband emerged from the house and beckoned to me. I climbed the few steps to his verandah where he thrust a huge glass of a pale, milky liquid into my hand – ouzo – the "national beverage". Although it was obvious there would be minimal verbal communication I declaimed "Notios Afriki" (South Africa) while pointing to self and company still munching mulberries in the garden. He asked "Notios Afriki?" and raised his eyebrows. I affirmed "Notios Afriki" nodding and smiling between gulps of ouzo. He retorted: "Notios Afriki boom boom". This mystified us. "Boom boom", what could this mean? It was only long afterwards that we heard that two bombs had been detonated in an urban centre in South Africa: boom boom! For all the lack of conversation there existed nevertheless a feeling of hospitality graciously offered and appreciatively received.

There is no overcrowding on the island if village population figures are anything to go by: Astris 62; Chrisi Akti 18; Thymonia 16; hill villages Mik, Prinos and Levki each swarm with 5 inhabitants, showing that Greece is following the world-wide trend of population drift to the cities. At Chrisi Akti we camped on the beach – literally on the sand – in a small pine grove which at that time was also harbouring two other camper vans. The beach sand was white and warm, the sea clear and cool, and these commodities were put to good use. On our second evening here we decided to dine at the nearby tavern which was gaily decorated with coloured lamps over an outdoor patio and bazouki strains from the interior. We selected an outdoor table under cover of reed matting and before you could say Hatzigiorgis we were tucking into souvlakia, salad and wine. Before long our waiter arrived at our table with another bottle of wine, not ordered by us. I was trying to convey this to him when he pointed meaningfully toward a Greek party dining several tables distant. One of the men-folk was celebrating his birthday and had apparently included us. We duly toasted him, looking momentarily like four Statues of Liberty, and yelled "afgheristo" (thank you). Within twenty minutes another bottle had arrived from him and soon after, a third! Although appreciative of his goodwill and amazing hospitality we were beginning to feel uneasy at this profusion of kindness, however the wine itself forestalled any serious concern. We thanked and toasted him each time a bottle arrived, which gestures he gallantly made little of.

Patrons were entertained by a number of young men who had formed a circle in a clearing between tables and began an impromptu folk-dance; linking arms and swaying first this way and then that to an exuberant Greek rhythm. These young men, in their twenties I'd guess, were utterly charming in their natural and spontaneous merrymaking without embarrassment or the slightest effeminacy. We remarked afterwards that such an event would be as rare as the proverbial "hen's teeth" in South Africa.

Further down the beach at Chrisi Akti were pedal boats for hire. This we could not resist and the next day found us on a four-seater, legs pumping and thrashing the water like a mini Mississippi paddle-steamer while heading out to sea. The sea-bed was visible for a long way out and it was rather exciting reaching the more voluptuous swell of deep water as the bay opened out. It was tempting to carry on towards the horizon in such fine weather. We had a vision of the boat-hire proprietor watching our receding craft with concern "… are those fools off to the islands, perhaps Turkey?" Of course he hadn't been watching us and was totally unconcerned when we arrived back, overdue.

The occasional sign on Thasos afforded us a chuckle. At Limenas a notice outside the police station quaintly advised: "Parking only for police's cars". Nearby, another warned: "No parking here for blocking the corner". This was displayed outside a "pension" (boarding house): "We rend rooms". A carry-over from the battle of the Titans? Another succinctly stated: "Furnitured rooms".

Overcast and chilly weather helped to tear us away from this Jewel of the Aegean and after returning to the mainland we regretfully decided that our steps would have to be directed westwards. We'd had the intention of making for Istanbul but this lay a further 500 kilometres to the east. Considering that the return journey would be made along the same route, it would thus be a journey of 1000+ kilometers – too far in distance and too long in time. Istanbul alias Constantinople alias Byzantium one-time eastern capital of the Roman Empire and seat of Orthodox Christianity would have to wait till next time.

Further inland, not far from Kavala, we visited the ruins of Philippi. Here we found an extensive archeological site, the remains of a large Greek city which was later added to by the Romans. A number of monumental Roman arches rise triumphantly over the ravages of Time – the "puller-down" of all things. This was also the setting for that historical showdown when Octavius Caesar and Mark Antony avenged Julius's assassination by defeating the armies of the main conspirators, Brutus and Cassius in 42 BC. A little to one side of the road which runs through the ruins one may see the cell where the apostle Paul had been imprisoned.

We now retraced our route as far as Thessaloniki before heading inland, bound for Meteora. A pleasant drive of a few hours through mountains and verdant indigenous forests brought us to a valley, where, breathless, we gazed at the majesty of gigantic rock formations soaring skywards. Sheer-sided cliffs known collectively as Meteora, rise hundreds of metres, their formation being something of a geological mystery. The summits of these granite monoliths were chosen by various persecuted Christian monks for their inaccessibility in the middle ages, and the staggering task of building monasteries was begun. Access for men and materials was provided by means of nets, ropes and winches which no doubt tested many a monk's faith while ascending or descending. Nowadays access has been provided by stairs hewn into the rock-face and bridges where necessary. Of twenty six monasteries so constructed only six have survived and are occupied by a mere handful of monks, often on a tour of duty from Mount Athos. Due to their aloof situation the monasteries were protected from the attentions of marauding Islamic invaders from Arabia and Turkey over the centuries. As a result of this "protection by position", most Byzantine frescoes and mosaics in the chapels are in near perfect condition. The monasteries provide exciting exploring and spectacular views across the valley abound. Artifacts, icons, relics and robes are on display including outstanding 10th century illuminated manuscripts.

At one of the monasteries Joanna found a locked door containing a peep-hole. As any good explorer would, she placed an eye to the aperture only to recoil with an audible gasp. Observing this, there was now no power on earth that could have prevented my own eye from fastening itself to the hole. In the gloomy half-light I beheld row upon row of human skulls stacked neatly one above the other, grinning in various stages of dental deficiency as if amused at the shock they occasioned.

Also present in the granite walls of Meteora are numbers of natural caves, scores of metres above the ground containing evidence of human habitation in some distant past.

Leaving Meteora we travelled westward, crossed the scenic Pindos mountain range and headed for Janena the capital of Epirus. Before reaching Janena however, we called in at the town of Perama, site of a now famous grotto accidently discovered during World War 2. The grotto (really an extensive subterranean cave network) was open to visitors and our uniformed guide, Captain Bill, showed us the extensive galleries where nature has depicted frozen motion where the centuries trickle by leaving barely susceptible alteration. Capt. Bill was one of those characters oozing personality and humour, and as we progressed into the bowels of the mountain he tested our knowledge of Greek, immediately coming to the conclusion that we were in urgent need of having our vocabularies broadened. His impromptu and rather dramatic technique was to suddenly turn on his single-filing charges (Peggy leading, had the full brunt of this), and utter a Greek word that we had to dutifully repeat, in unison, syllable by laboured syllable until his expected standard of proficiency was achieved. "Glis – ther – a", Captain Bill would bark while indicating the concept "slippery" by rubbing the sole of his shoe back and forth across a wet stone.. When this was pronounced to his satisfaction, we moved on, only to be pulled up sharply with "spe – le – os" accompanied by a vague wave indicating the cavern. At times the situation seemed so utterly insane and bizarre that the politely suppressed laughter threatened to explode into hysterical shrieking and general falling about. We managed to stave off mental breakdown however, and happily treated Captain Bill to a Greek coffee and cake at tour's end.

We had been moving in a large circular sweep through the Greek interior and at Janena we found a good campsite and had supper at an enchanting restaurant on the bank of a small lake which sparkled with the reflection of the myriad lights along the shore. Our inexperience in the ordering of food showed up when requesting a plate of "mezze" (starters) for each one of us. No wonder the waiter gave us a quizzical look - mezze is one plate shared among the company!

Our next destination lay southeast to the navel of the classical world – Delphi. Zeus, says the legend, released two eagles in opposite directions until they met over this place, the navel or centre of the earth, which would become the most sacred sanctuary of ancient times. Sited on a rugged slope of Mount Parnassus overlooking a valley of olive trees, the Gulf of Itea glittered fifteen kilometers to the south. Delphi is said to be the next most important archeological site after the acropolis in Athens, home to the Parthenon, and was originally dedicated to the goddess Gaia, Mother of All. This honour was later transferred to Apollo, a god of many attributes: beauty, clarity of mind, the foundation of cities, aversion of evil, power of the sun, and more. Worshippers were served by a succession of oracles from 2500 BC until the Christian Emperor Theodosius felt that enough was enough and in 394 AD banned all so-called pagan worship. The dolphin was sacred to Apollo and the word appears to be cognate with Delphi.

This remarkable sanctuary reached its peak as a religious centre in 600 BC and pilgrims came from near and far (as they do today) for spiritual upliftment. The oracle was seated in the holy of holies in the Temple of Apollo and made her predictions and advice in a strange tongue upon the inhalation of mystical fumes emanating from a cleft in the rock. This required interpretation by temple priests. It is told that the Athenian leaders sought her advice when the Persian hordes were advancing on the city having by-passed Thermopylae (held by 300 Spartans) to avenge their defeat at Marathon. The oracles message was gloomy: "All is ruined, for fire and the god of war speeding headlong in a Syrian chariot shall bring you low". This portent stimulated the Athenians to much prayer and supplication to the goddess Athena; this had the effect of eliciting a revised communication from the oracle: "The wooden wall shall not fall, but will help you and your children". This mysterious advice was interpreted by the Greek commander Themistocles to mean that they should seek a sea battle with the Persians, the "wooden walls" being the hulls of their ships. The Athenian population was evacuated, the Persians razed the city but the Athenian navy subsequently trounced the Persian fleet at the famous sea battle of Salamis.

Important civic and political questions were referred to the oracle. On one occasion Socrates was informed, via the oracle, that there was no man alive wiser than he. This puzzled the enlightened philosopher enough to set him in search of someone wiser than himself to test the veracity of the oracle. However Socrates bequeathed to posterity, through his chronicler Plato, the wonderful dialogues wherein he questioned the self-styled wise of Athens and elsewhere only to find, to their chagrin, that they were not wise after all. Socrates was thus unable to refute the oracle on this point.

In the "pronaos", or foyer, of the Temple to Apollo stood the bust of the great poet Homer and inscribed on the walls were the famous philosophical dicta: "Know thyself"; "Nothing in excess". A retaining wall forming a plinth to the temple is faced with un-jointed, perfectly fitting, polygonal stonework, unlike later Roman masonry which required mortared joints due to imperfections in the stone edging. Notable Greek honours and exploits were engraved on this polygonal wall. Many smaller temples and treasuries containing votive offerings from various city-states line the broad path which leads to the Temple of Apollo known as the Sacred Way. Above the Temple is an amphitheatre set in wooded surroundings and above this again, a gymnasium in an excellent state of preservation. Nearby we drank, washed face and hands at the Castalian Spring, now piped down to the roadside. This water was said to be holy and pilgrims were required to clean and purify themselves before entering the sanctuary. The spring water was in ancient times ducted to the oracle's chamber and was said to have the power of bestowing on mankind poetic inspiration and prophesy. We also rambled through ruins of a lesser sanctuary, below the main Temple, dedicated to Pronaia Athena which was visited by pilgrims prior to entering the Temple of Apollo. Superb architectural remains exist in Athena's precincts, not least of which is a partly reconstructed Tholos, a circular colonnaded structure of great delicacy thought to have mystical siginificance. We were reminded of the Tholos at the wellness-centre (Asclepia) at Epidauros.

There is undoubtedly a strong "atmosphere" in Delphi as if the accumulated veneration over millennia has lingered among the fallen stones – even trodden into the very ground by the millions of footsteps that have converged on this place. As an unforgettable manifestation of all powerful Energy, a fierce wind-storm swept across the mountains and that night in camp the wind-god robbed us of sleep as the camper was rocked by great buffetings, and the girls likewise, as he snatched and tugged at their tent. Earlier, prior to us returning to camp, the eyelet securing the main guy-rope had been ripped out of the nylon flysheet by the wind. An anonymous camper had retied the rope in our absence and I felt at the time that it was these thoughtful kindnesses that serve to unite the camping fraternity.

In the archeological museum at Delphi there is much to be appreciated and among the fine examples of statuary is the famous "charioteer", a superb bronze in perfect condition whose eyes alone are masterpieces of white enamel and onyx. From the sublime to the ridiculous, a notice at the entrance to the museum warns the public: "It is forbidden to take photos of visitors in the museum".

Not everyone has found Delphi congenial. Aesop (of the Fables) had visited the sanctuary and was returning home when a golden chalice was found to be missing under circumstances that pointed to Aesop possibly being the guilty party. He was hauled back to Delphi protesting his innocence; summarily tried; found guilty and executed by being hurled off a cliff. Later the chalice was found – it had been mislaid! Unfortunately Aesop was unable to formulate a moral to the story.

On the road once again, we headed for the Corinthian canal via Athens where we were expecting mail. We had been keeping in touch with "the folks back home" by advising them to write care of the "poste restante" counter of the main post offices in the cities we considered we would be passing through about a month later. The system worked fairly well and we supplemented our communications with the occasional phone call. (Some countries had direct dialing facilities in call boxes). This time however, we were awaiting a rather special letter.

Our son Mark, not in a position to accompany us at the start of the trip, had at the end of April, some two months after our departure flown to London where he met up with South African friends. It had been pre-arranged that he would join us on our travels, but how to make contact? Through Mark's grandparents in Durban we obtained his address in London. We wrote to Mark and suggested he meet us in Rome on, say, 14th June. He was to immediately reply care of poste-restante Rome advising where in Rome he would wait to meet us on that day, only ten days off. Would it work? We would have to be in Rome by then, find the correct poste-restante post office, collect his letter and from his description locate the address where he would be waiting for us. In Rome!

Passing through the village of Eleusis about 21 kilometres west of Athens, we felt we could not miss the chance for a peep at the ancient site where the sacred rites known as the Eleusian Mysteries were performed. As it turned out all we did have was, literally, a peep. On Sunday afternoons archeological sites close at 3 pm. We discovered this at 3:05 pm. The best we could do was to wander along the fence peering at the ruins in the middle distance. We considered it to be an Eleusian Mystery why the site had to be closed at this early hour with at least 5 hours of daylight left!

Next day we drove back into the hurly-burly of Athens but, no mail. We headed for the Canal and beyond to our point of departure for Italy, Patras; our point of arrival some 5 weeks earlier. But before then, there was one other ancient settlement to be visited in the Peloponnese – Mycenae. Along with nearby Tiryns, it is the most ancient site yet discovered in Greece. It meant a detour, but we were not in a hurry to leave Greece.

Mycenae – the name evokes ghostly images that drift uncertainly across an aeon from their origin in pre-history, swathed in legend and myth. Perseus, son of Zeus, was said to have founded a dynasty here in 1700 BC. He is also remembered for slaying Medusa, one of the gorgons, by using his shield as a mirror in which he could observe the lady with serpents for hair, without becoming petrified. Today Mycenae has been extensively excavated and digging continues. It is a stirring experience to walk up the paved incline on the acropolis, flanked by walls constructed of huge 5 ton "Cyclopean" blocks of dressed stone, through the Lion Gate and into King Agamemnon's palace. This famous gateway is of lintel and post construction forming a square opening of about 3 metres. Above the lintel is a huge bas-relief of two opposing lionesses in upright, profiled stance with fore-feet resting on a plinth bearing a central column, faces turned enquiringly towards the approacher. Beyond the gate lay the burial ground and then the palace. The palace is outlined by the remains of walls and the floor tiling to the "megaron" (throne room) is in remarkably good shape after three and a half millennia. In times of siege water was obtained from the "Spring of Perseus" and stored in a cistern hewn deep in the bedrock. We descended the hundred or so steps down to the cistern in pitch blackness relieved only by the lighting of a candle stub we had found at the shaft entrance. On the floor of the rubble-filled cistern we found a perfectly good copy of a Greek guide book – in German. Was a German tourist lying trapped beneath the rubble as a result of a rock-fall? Had Agamemnon's ghost appeared out of the cistern causing a German tourist to abandon all encumbrances in his headlong flight to the surface? It was clearly time to leave and to the accompaniment of giggles and shrieks we ascended the rock stairway to the blinding glare of a midday sun. We were intrigued by the royal grave circle where golden treasure was found, including the death mask conjectured to have been Agamemnon's, now located in the archeological museum in Athens.

The discovery of the tombs was an archeologists dream. They were unearthed by an amateur German archeologist by name of Schliemann in 1876. One can, or perhaps not, imagine his feelings as he brought nineteen skeletons to the surface, as well as 14 kilograms of golden objects which had been embedded for thirty five centuries. This discovery was the first direct evidence of the legendary Mycenaean civilization referred to by Homer in his epic poems. Nine gigantic "bee-hive" tombs were also discovered and the largest of these was the final resting place of King Agamemnon's progenitor King Atreus. Known as the "Treasury of Atreus", this circular tomb is a colossal 13 metres high inside with a diameter of 15 metres at the base. An imposing passageway, now open to the sky, 14 metres long and 6 wide leads to the doorway of the underground tomb where an 8 metre long slab of stone, estimated to weigh 120 tons, serves as a lintel. The elliptical or "bee-hive" dome was built in "dry-wall" manner with neatly laid corbelling of tightly fitting flat stones. An acoustical peculiarity exists directly below the apex of the roof. If a sharp sound is made, a clap of hands or stamp of foot, a reverberating echo is heard. Leading off the main vault is a small rectangular chamber, supposedly the actual burial place. There can be no finer panegyric to that engineer way back in 1350 BC than the excellent structural condition of this tomb. Other bee-hive tombs have not fared as well and have partially collapsed. One American lady visitor remarked in a voice audible to all within the tomb: "But where are the windows?" Her companion, after a brief stunned silence, drawled: "Darling... this is a tomb! They put dead people in here".

The heat was blistering when we returned to the camper, and on opening the doors a vast contingent of giant flies, who appeared to have been awaiting this moment, swarmed into the shade within the vehicle. It was uncanny. There was hardly an area larger than a dinner plate that was not accommodating at least one fly in an attitude of tranquil repose. At first we tried shoo-ing them out. This merely stirred them into a loud buzzing until we stopped shoo-ing at which they resumed their state of tranquil trespass. After a few ineffective attempts at forceful eviction, we decided to drive off with the side door open. In conjunction with the suction caused by the slipstream, Peggy and the girls contrived to remove the unwelcome squatters. We must have left a wake of confused flies kilometers long. However we would no sooner consider that we had been 100% successful when another little fellow would emerge. He would be cajoled to a side window which would be rapidly wound down and another fly was whisked out of our van and our lives. That night was to be our final night in Greece and we enjoyed a last swim in the Gulf of Corinth from our campsite near Patras. The next day we recalled the mournful expressions on the faces of the travelers leaving Greece and wondered if newcomers saw similar expressions on our faces as we glumly waited for boarding time on the dockside, having in turn been infected by the soul of Greece.

We stood at the stern rail wistfully watching Greece sliding away into the hazy distance, while being ferried back to Brindisi, Italy. Again, we had contrived to place the camper alongside the starboard rail and once more felt like 1st class passengers. During the voyage we saw a number of vessels, probably ferries as this was a popular route. After nightfall we enjoyed watching the ships' lights in the dark distance. The journey was almost too long for a number of passengers, me included, due to the pitching, yawing and rolling of the boat, which motions combine into a track the shape of a corkscrew. We were pushing into a lumpy sea and fresh headwind, and there was a noticeable falling off of appetite.

BACK TO ITALY

After disembarking, our journey continued along the "arch" of the "boot" that is Italy through flat countryside until we reached Crotone, where we camped "wild" on a red-sanded beach due to a shortage of campsites in the area. We came across an ancient Greek temple nearby (dedicated to the goddess Hera) and realized that the Greek influence was still with us. Southern Italy had been colonized by the Greeks from about 750 BC and in numbers sufficient for the area to be called Magna Graecia.

We had now to decide whether to press on southwards to Sicily – an alluring prospect – or cut across to the west coast and head north. As we were committed to meeting Mark in 5 days, we decided that time was insufficient to do the island justice, and Sicily went onto the "next-time" list. From Crotone to Cosenza on the west coast the road traverses alpine landscape with lush wild-flowered meadows, streams and many road tunnels. One of these tunnels will be remembered by us for a very long time.

Shortly after entering this particular tunnel – headlamps on as is obligatory for all vehicles passing through tunnels – we noticed an approaching car, by its headlights, to be occupying the same lane as ourselves. The vehicle then swerved back into its correct side of the road, but seconds later moved across into our lane again. At this stage I began steadily flashing the bright beams (never thought of the hazard lights) and started easing up on the accelerator. It was no use sounding the horn as it had given up the ghost on the second day of our travels. The tunnel suddenly seemed a small place to be in: a steel guard-rail on the right and to the left a solid white barrier line marking the centre of the road. The gap between the camper and the oncoming lunatic was closing rapidly and we could clearly see approaching traffic beyond him. This precluded a last-second swerve into the adjacent lane. A battery of headlamps now filled the tunnel. I flashed the "brights" more rapidly and started braking. Closer and closer rushed the headlamps. At the same time that Peggy screamed "JESUS" the oncoming car veered across to its own side of the road, barely missing us, and flashed by. What possessed the other driver will forever remain a mystery, but the relief felt by us in the seconds following was palpable. This incident was an hors- d'oeuvre to a feast of Italian west coast driving that must have had the Grim Reaper drooling with expectation.

The coastal road clings tenuously to a mountainside and hairpin bends have been carved into the rock-face which soars hundreds of metres above a lace-fringed sea. Breathtaking views vied with maniacal drivers for our attention as along these twisting asphalt ribbons the Italians hurtled each attempting to emulate, or so it seemed, a formula-one driver at work. A perfunctory "beep" on his horn preceded a sudden manifestation of car/truck/bus whipping round a blind corner, and neither the absence of forward visibility nor presence of solid barrier line had the least effect in moderating their speed or preventing overtaking in circumstances one kilometer per hour short of disaster.

We booked into an attractive campsite near the beach at the town of Sapri, and decided it was high time we ate out again. We had always sampled local restaurants at least once in each country as budget restrictions prevented regular dining out, The honour now fell on a small restaurant near the beach. At the outset it was clear that there was a language problem and I "non-comprehended" at a rate thus far unequalled on the trip. Our culinary desire was a fish and/or pasta dish, hopefully of a local character. We accordingly ordered the "pesce con pasta" for a price thought to be about L6000 each (R4,80). The kitchen throbbed into life (we were the only guests – why did this not warn us?). A tablecloth appeared and soon the drinks were brought. The congenial atmosphere diminished slightly when plates of spaghetti arrived, smothered in what looked like tomato paste. A whispered "What happened to the fish?" The spaghetti proved to be edible although there were doubts at times. After the plates had been cleared we wondered whether anything else was going to happen. It did – the evening's piece d' resistance arrived. On each plate was a curious collection of, presumably, "fruits of the sea". Small, white, multi-limbed squid jostled against a few prawns and less identifiable objects.

Bleak glances were exchanged as we mumbled "Grazie" with as much grace as memory of the spaghetti course permitted.

At this point self-control began disintegrating and muffled giggles developed into mild hysteria. Two things puzzled me however. One, the fact that, like the fabulous cornucopia, however much I consumed there remained a never-diminishing heap of pathetic looking little squid, their twisted tentacles pointing accusingly in all directions as if uncertain whom to blame for their predicament; or perhaps blaming us all! That Peggy, Melody and Joanna coped so well with their rubbery squid was the other puzzle. Was there a connection between this "mystery" and the furtive shuffling that animated the ladies whenever I happened to glance away from the table? The scene which followed when a bill was presented showing an amount at least twice what we had been expecting, including mandatory "tip", extinguished the humour of the occasion.

Further up the coast we visited the ancient Greek settlement of Paestum. This ruined city, about two kilometers across, boasts straight roads paved with great basalt blocks, often showing grooved wheel ruts. At intersections, two stepping-stones were strategically placed to allow pedestrians to cross without actually stepping on the roadway which doubled as a drain. Wagon and chariot wheels passed between the outer gaps between the stones, suggesting standardization of wheel gauges among cartwrights. The main Temple of Poseidon ("Neptune", to the Romans) is one of the most complete extant ancient Greek structures. Apart from the roof, an odd frieze or "metope", every column, lintel and pediment is in place and in fair condition. The Temple is a huge and majestic building dating from the 5th century BC. It was thrilling to wander through and between the ancient market squares, public baths, houses and other ruined buildings whose walls in many places exist up to window sill level. Much of the city is inaccessible due to the sheer mass of undergrowth covering the ruins. A sign at the entrance which we only happened to see as we were leaving sternly warned the visitor that: "It is forbidden to climb up the ancient walls and over enclosures. The management declines all responsibility of eventual accidents. In case of damage, the transgressors will be denounced". I had in fact transgressed and almost been denounced, unaware of it at the time, while clambering across several walls when an attendant some distance away brought the full fury of his whistle to bear on me as he gesticulated furiously that I should keep off the ruins. I was indeed fortunate that I had caused no damage!

A little further on, just beyond Salerno but this side of Naples, a promontory juts into the sea. It is shaped very like a clenched hand with index finger extended, similar to the old-fashioned sign telling you where the "gents" is, or the ticket office. This terrestrial index finger points straight to an island a few kilometers offshore known as Capri (not to be missed say the books). We drove onto the clenched hand, the promontory, from the base of the wrist towards the little finger on the Drive called Amalfi. The road lies at the foot of a mountain and is justly famous for its spectacular scenery; the sea surging against the cliffs below. Small villages and resorts cling to the mountainside as the road dips down into and across great ravines which open out in pretty bays, sometimes a sandy beach, always with colourful fishing boats tethered to the seabed. An occasional open, horse-drawn carriage clip-clopped along the waterfront, a reminder of a bygone day when life moved at a gracious pace. It was dark when we reached the campsite at Sorrento, half-way along the top of the index finger. Exploration would have to wait till the morrow.

The shoreline along Sorrento comprises a 30 metre high sheer cliff face. We parked the camper and walked down a long flight of steps to a tiny harbor where a ferry would convey us to the romantic Isola di Capri and the Blue Grotto. A launch took half-an hour to reach the harbor at Capri and we were mildly surprised to find that we had to transfer to another ferry. We followed the island's rugged coastline in a smaller launch and after 15 minutes arrived at the famous sea-cave, and beheld a strange sight.

About a dozen small row-boats were eagerly awaiting the arrival of the Capri ferries. They were clustered in the lee of a promontory like an ambuscade. As our ferry arrived, a number of row-boats would peel off from the general flotilla and come alongside, to do business. Passengers were urged by voice and gesture to transfer to the smaller vessel. A combination of factors such as: a running swell; the advanced age of several tourists; ladies' impractical footwear and tight skirts; general muttered misgivings about the whole thing as expressed by the more timid souls; all these things made the operation of transferring to the row-boats highly entertaining. With nothing more than a few yelps from our ladies (the unspoken fear of course being that the boats would drift apart at precisely the moment that one has a foot in each). We secured our places and in convoy with several other boats were rowed to a small opening in the cliff-face. The state of the tide was such that the opening was just large enough to admit the passage of a row-boat provided that the oarsman: shipped his oars at the last minute; grabbed hold of a chain running through the opening; exhorted his passengers to crouch into the bilge (to avoid a head injury); and tug manfully on the chain to gather momentum for the boat to coast into the grotto.

An eerie, pale light permeates the grotto which is about 30 metres deep, half as wide and four or five metres high above the water level. It is the water itself which creates a feeling of "other-worldliness". Daylight appears to be reflected off a white sea-floor some 20 metres below, rising as a transparent glow which swathes the hulls of the boats, oars and trailed fingers like an azure aura. The overall impression likened to floating across a surrealistic, glowing fluorescent-tube.

It was rather unfortunate that our collective "gondoliers" felt it necessary to "improve" the atmosphere by lusty renderings of "Arividerci Roma" and similar outpourings; the vocalists in other row-boats seemingly oblivious of their competitors (or determined to out-sing them). The resulting cacophony of Italian counterpoint resonating through the grotto completed the fantasy. Minutes later we were back outside – with vibrating psyches – awaiting the ferry. Our musical matelote left us in no doubt that he would not be embarrassed by being offered a "tip". In fact he indicated that the size of the tip should take into account that there were four of us in his charge.

Back at Capri harbour, we caught the funicular railway up the terraced hillside. At the top there is a pretty square, decorated with flowering shrubs and offering magnificent views across the island, harbour and sea. We rambled through the town enjoying the sights, sounds and smells of a busy commercial area, and the calm peacefulness of the residential parts where white-washed villas presented geraniums, bougainvillea and wisteria. Too soon it was time to leave for the mainland and we wended our way back to the harbour.

An off-shore breeze had arisen which for us, returning to the mainland, proved to be a fresh headwind. Blissfully disregarding this circumstance we seated ourselves on the fore-deck of the motor launch for the return journey to Sorrento. As the boat left the shelter of the harbour and turned into wind, there arose a feeling in us that our seating arrangement had not been wisely chosen. The feeling became tangible as a sizeable sheet of sea spurted over the windward rail. This had the effect of clearing the deck of most of the passengers who retired to the dry safety of the cabin. We, and another hardy couple, had the fore-deck, and what was in store for us, to ourselves. The other man wore a peaked "skippers" cap at a jaunty angle and probably felt that having donned the symbol he was obliged to man his post. His lady wore, appropriately, a swimming costume. The boat settled into rhythmical pitching, rising on the swell and plunging into the following trough and each time sending a plume of briny across the bow. Within minutes we were saturated and as we could become no wetter it became rather fun. We were not unhappy however when a half-hour later we chugged into the protection of Sorrento harbour. It was a matter of small concern to find a parking ticket attached to the camper on our return – the trifles of man seemed petty after Dealing with the Sea – and the ticket was promptly consigned to the souvenir box.

We changed into dry clothes and with a few hours of daylight remaining decided to drive on to Pompeii. Up to AD 79 Pompeii had been a sea-port of some notoriety. In that fateful year Mount Vesuvius, a few kilometres to the north-east, spewed out death and destruction and deposited enough material to drive the sea back by about two kilometers, which is where the coastline stands today. We found an attractive campsite across the road from the vast archeological excavations which is ancient Pompeii. Although a railway track lay behind the campsite the fruiting apricot trees compensated for this. Regularly the air would fill with rumbling thunder and the ground would shake – were we back in 79 AD? Aware of the proximity of Vesuvius, the passing of trains was made more acceptable by knowing that the great dragon was still resting. The ladies discovered a bath-tub in their ablution block – the only bath encountered in the 101 campsites that we would stay in on this trip. The ladies lingered long and luxuriously in the tub (one at a time of course), no doubt recalling the mod.cons. of far-off domestic days.

We made an early start next day to explore the ancient city, and passing through one of the city gates were pulled up by the following sign:

THE RUINS MANAGEMENT

Invites all visitors to step carefully through the ruins, in order to avoid unpleasant accidents. The environment is in fact uncomfortable and the ruins are not good for your safely.

The environment may well have been uncomfortable to the original inhabitants, perhaps even to the author of the sign, but we found it exciting, stimulating and awesome. Imagine a city of thousands, blanketed almost instantaneously by layers of stones, dust and hot ash up to six metres deep, thereby "freezing" the entire city in all its living attitudes until opened up 1700 years later. Here is a city that was not destroyed by a conquering invader nor razed by fire or earthquake. In fact Pompeii could not have been better preserved from the ravages of time or man for the fascination of posterity and the special interest of archeologists than by its "hermetically" sealed encapsulation.

Houses, temples, shops, theatres, baths, bakeries, storerooms together with their contents – amphorae, ornaments, pottery, glass phials, stone measuring weights, jewelry, even a store of dried fish – have been exposed with new finds coming to light as the remainder of the city, roughly a third, bows to the pick and trowel. Delicate bronze statues and colourful frescoes, magnificent mosaic floors and marble sculptures again present themselves for the delight of all who examine them.

A pathetic note is sounded by the plaster casts of human and animal figures, the sight of which evokes a sense of the disaster and immediacy of events even though separated by centuries. These casts portray figures in various attitudes: a couple embracing or shielding a child, arms raised to ward off the hot rain of death; the resigned acceptance which a quiet posture with knees drawn up in a foetal position seems to portray. Such tragic tableaux were preserved by the ingenious method of pouring plaster into the voids formed in the volcanic deposits by creatures whose bodies had eventually decomposed leaving a "natural" mould.

Buildings have been catalogued according to their function or ownership as construed by discovered evidence. Descriptive names have been given.

There are: the "House of the Surgeon" where ancient surgical instruments were unearthed; the "Court of the Gladiators" where eighteen skeletons were found in two rooms -one of whom was richly adorned in jewels, as well as gladiator's weapons and helmets; the "House of the Lovers" so named after graffiti in a mural reading: "Lovers, like bees, make life as sweet as honey"; the "House of the Faun" - here was found, decorating an ornamental pond, a bronze miniature of an exquisitely graceful dancing faun; and a little unexpectedly: the "House of the Moralist", so called as the owner had adorned the walls with the following maxims: "The servant shall wash and dry the feet of the guest"; "A cloth must protect the cushions and the linen must be well cared for"; "Abandon lascivious looks and do not cast sweet glances at the women of others"; "Be chaste in speech"; "Abstain from anger if possible, if not, return to your own home".

Rather balefully overlooking the city, Mount Vesuvius stands as a perpetual reminder of the devastation delivered to Pompeii and nearby Herculaneum (not open to the public due to excavations underway). Vesuvius was a "pot brought to the boil" in AD 79, has "boiled over" on other occasions since, and as we discovered when visiting the mountain, was still "simmering". At the parking lot where we would leave the camper, we were informed that guides and boots were mandatory and both could be hired. With the boots came a pair of disposable plastic bags, in the shape of socks, to provide protection against the microbiological possibilities investing the boots from the previous hirer. The guide was a grizzled old character whose complexion blended with the reddish brown of the volcanic surroundings. A path led to the summit a few hundred metres higher in a landscape of total desolation – sterile lava and vitrified clinker glinted weakly in the sunlight. At the summit, 1277 metres above sea level, the undoubtedly magnificent view over surrounding land and sea was denied us by the haze present. However the "action" lay in the crater where along the rim, active fumaroles puffed steam rather forbiddingly. We had freed ourselves from the guide by the simple expedient of providing the expected tip. He adjured us to be careful, reminded us that the last eruption was in 1944, and then moved on to fresh pastures while we soaked up "atmosphere". Attentive listening across the crater, perhaps 800 metres in diameter, discerned the faint crackling of stressed rock faces. The original crater of AD 79 is still visible below and to the west of the present crater, and stands as a curving ridge about 7 kilometres in diameter. We had the notion that we had the effrontery to climb an earth-dragon's back whilst it was slumbering. Decidedly not a good place to be if he awoke!

Sunday afternoon and Sunday traffic with a vengeance. We were inching along the main road towards Naples in company with thousands of similarly inching cars. Enterprising youngsters had set up cold-drink stands on the roadside and were doing a roaring trade with the captive motoring population creeping by. I decided to exit from the procession and wait for the traffic to clear and noticed a parking area which seemed suitable. I had been suffering from a mild attack of "people claustrophobia" in the flow of traffic, but no relief was to be found in the parking ground. A large number of youths were chasing each other in the area at a breakneck pace. Others were attempting to charm young girls lounging in small knots who appeared to have nothing better to do than stand around smoking. When these entertainments began to pall, they would visit the camper and try to elicit (Italian) conversation from its apparently backward occupants. We were saved by a diversion from a noisy gathering nearby. A stout gentleman in a vest and dark trousers appeared to be intent on throttling an equally large lady wearing a black dress. This scenario was attended by a number of men and women, possibly relatives, who eventually and with much excitability, managed to prevail on the throttler to desist. The crowd dispersed after the woman removed herself amid threats and counter-threats between factions in the crowd.

We had not seen a bakery and I was given the task of seeking out the "staff of life". I recalled seeing vendors in the road offering what might have been foodstuffs to the occupants of cars in the turgid traffic flow, and decided to investigate. Within a few hundred metres I came across a vendor, ascertained that his produce was wheaten and selling at "millelire" (one thousand lire – about 80 cents) per packet. In the best tourist tradition and in a unique imitation of Italian, I haggled the price down to 400 lire (or so I thought). Sensing that my offer had been accepted I drew out my wallet and started peeling off 1000 lire notes. After 4000 lire had changed hands, I turned away clutching my purchase and marched off with the confident tread of one who has Bartered Successfully. I had almost reached the camper when I realized with a jolt that stopped me in my tracks: I had overpaid by a factor of 10: 4000 lire instead of 400 lire! Swinging around I saw the rapidly retreating figure of the vendor. Ruefully I returned to the camper where I was subjected to great heaps of well-deserved scorn when I related the circumstances of the transaction; and seconds later fresh heaps when it was discovered that the packet contained, instead of the bread-sticks I was expecting, a rather insipid looking pile of baby-biscuits. Months later I would again be reminded of this "faux pas" when discovering the biscuits in the deepest reach of the food store – they had never even been eaten!

There is an expression: "See Naples and Die". Presumably this refers to the notion that Naples is of such unparalleled beauty that there is no good reason to continue living after visiting this city as nothing worth seeing would ever be encountered thereafter. This was not our experience of Naples. In fact Naples seemed to us to embody much of the noise, congestion, squalidness (in parts), driving hysteria and general sense of anarchy which typifies south-western Italy. We did not wish to remain long in the city and after lunch at the small-craft harbour drove to well-signposted Pozzuoli. This volcanic crater with its active fumaroles presents an unearthly scene. The crater floor is at ground level, about 600 metres in diameter, and is encircled by a low, ragged ridge of earth. The yellowish crusty surface in the crater is devoid of life due to the profusion of sulphurous fumaroles puffing and wheezing spasmodically. A large area is fenced off with a notice to: "Keep Clear - Flying Stones". Within this enclosure there are large pits of bubbling mud, spurting clouds of steam. Many boulders have evidently "flown" judging from the disposition of rocks littering the area, some the size of grapefruit. Elsewhere fissures in the ground were thickly encrusted with sulphur and the steam emerging too hot for the hand to be held near. One particular funnel-shaped crevice roared like a Primus stove. The "rotten egg" smell of sulphur caused a few crinkled noses but one soon became accustomed to it. Indeed, it was not unpleasant to enter a low brick tunnel built over a particularly fierce blast from the nether world as a kind of sulphurous sauna, and crouch in the heat while marveling at the fantastic crystalline formations on the rough edges of the tunnel surface: multi-faceted whites, yellows and golds; needles and wickers; star-clusters and feathers. It did occur to us that we were tramping about on the lid of an enormous steam-pot, but what the heck, the safety valves seemed to be working.

The following day we had arranged to meet our son, Mark, in Rome. He had not confirmed our rendezvous proposal and we were skeptical about the prospect of a successful reunion. Had he received our letter? Had he replied poste-restante Rome? How would he get to Rome? Where would we meet in this metropolis? These and other alarmist parental questions nibbled at our mind as we decided to head directly for Rome via the autopista.

Eternal Rome, June 15. We had arrived the previous evening with some trepidation as to whether we would find one of the several campsites in the city. This was actually easily accomplished because Rome has a ring road from which well-signposted feeder roads lead into the city. Our site lay close to the ring road which meant two buses into town (no way was I going to drive into the CBD). Having settled in, we made our way by public transport to the poste-restante ("posta-in-firma" in Italy) counter of the main post office. Bingo! a letter from Mark: "I will meet you at the Piazza del Republicana on June 15 as arranged and will wait there each day for 3 days". Hastily consulting our street map we made our way to the Piazza and ….."Yes, there he is!"

Mark had taken a coach from London and had arrived in Rome, as we had, the previous afternoon. We were thrilled at the success of the plan and celebrated the occasion over drinks at an up-market restaurant in the Piazza at a cost of one night's accommodation for the lot of us. Needless to say it was only one "round". We duly fetched Mark's luggage from the "pension" where he had stayed the previous night and left it at the rail station luggage store while we "sight-saw".

Rome is a lively city. Most buildings are of "monumental" design with baroque ornamentation typical of the older European cities, along with a patina of grime thanks to the advent of the internal combustion engine. Like Athens, a feeling of antiquity hangs over Rome, but unlike Athens where civic business in ancient times was conducted in the precincts of the acropolis and agora, Roman antiquities are scattered over a large area. However in the Imperial Forum and Capitoline Hill there is much to see: statues, triumphal arches; columns and other immodest extravagances erected by emperors: Julius Caesar, Hadrian, Trajan and their successors seeking immortality. Trajan's column is carved with his military exploits and the chiselled letters of the Roman text are a calligrapher's delight. The Capitol, or Capitoline Hill, comprises a harmonious arrangement of buildings sited on three sides of an ornamental square with statues, staircases and paving blending into a unified whole. The man largely responsible for this large-scale artwork is Michelangelo who received this commission in the 16th century. The significance of the Capitol site goes back to about 900 BC when, being the highest of the seven hills upon which Rome was to be built, this area was reserved for temples dedicated to the tutelary gods of the city.

It is very stimulating when the shadow of antiquity passes over one while standing amongst the ancient constructions. For a brief instant the dense veil of centuries past parts a little, and the beat of the drum, the tramp of mighty Roman legions, the smell of hot dust – a sense of History suddenly engulfs one. It is a marvel that so much has remained for so long. The "schlossen" on the Rhine (mostly decayed); the "chateaux" on the Loire (mostly restored); these are but yesterday's toys. Of course everything occupies its appointed place in the long march of the ages and Greek and Roman structures are but yesterday's toys next to Egypt's pyramids and sphinx.

One of the better preserved Roman edifices is the virtually intact Pantheon – dedicated to all the gods. But for sheer grandeur of construction the Colosseum surely has no rival in Rome. Tier upon tier of arched galleries rise into the sky which, in their day, accommodated 50 000 spectators who arrived from far and wide to be entertained. Typical activities were: duels by gladiators; hunting tableaux complete with created hills, streams, trees and, of course, the wild animals who were to be sacrificed to the god Amusement; naval battles with real ships for which purpose the entire arena was flooded; or to their everlasting shame, the systematic murder of the early Christians who had the audacity to pledge their allegiance to one they considered to be higher than the current emperor. The Roman military engineers, (forerunners of the species to become known as civilian or "civil" engineers) were without peer for those times. Many of their constructions are yet in daily use in areas dominated by the Roman Empire: arches; roads; bridges; aqueducts and viaducts; all testify to knowledge of design principles and behavior of construction materials.

Volcanic ash from Pozzuoli was a constituent of their cement and this additive, known as pozzolana, is still used today in building construction.

Leaving the ancient CBD we set out to explore the city. The tourist-haunted Trevi Fountain, where a giant Neptune stands imperiously in a chariot drawn by Tritons (his sons of the sea) as water cascades frothily all around, is situated in an incongruously small square. This adds an intimate charm to the scene as smiling tourists shuffle forward to be photographed in the company of the King of the Deep. From the floor of the basin in front of the fountain the sun twinkled in reflection from numerous coins that had been thrown in (back must be turned towards Neptune) to bribe the god to facilitate the thrower's return to Rome one day.

We meandered down the stylishly affected Via Vittorio Veneto but were better pleased to find a little Capuchin monastery down a side street. Here 18th century monks had demonstrated their talents by using human bones to bizarrely form montages on walls and ceilings. Great rose-patterns of scapulas (shoulder blades); butterflies of pelvises; vine-like tracery of spinal vertebrae; sprays of rib, arm and leg bones in kaleidoscopic array were the deadly décor. Stacked against the rear wall are row upon row of human skulls, staring vacantly at the visitor. In mute attendance stand a number of skeletons dressed in monks' robes, their bleached skulls grinning mirthlessly beneath their cowls. A skeleton had been meaningfully arranged on a ceiling, who in an outstretched hand carries a pair of weighing scales and in the other a scythe, all constructed from various bones of the body. The materials for this osseous collection had been supplied from the centuries' passing of resident monks who now enjoyed a kind of fragmented immortality.

Continuing along the Via Veneto we reached Rome's largest park, the Villa Borghese. Here we rested weary legs, took refreshment, and were entertained by Mark effecting the rescue of a model aeroplane which had power-dived into a tree and then be effusively thanked by its young Roman owner. As we strolled across the lawns the epithet "hot Latins" was verified by the sight of couples in tight clinches at regular intervals. We left the park at the Spanish Steps, a long and wide staircase overlooked by a 16th century French church. In front of the steps, a little incongruously, stood an Egyptian obelisk. A large crowd had assembled on the Steps to hear and enjoy a group of musicians performing on one of the larger landings so we joined them for a pleasant half-hour in the sun.

It is an attractive feature of many European cities that "busking", or impromptu pavement entertainment, is tolerated by the authorities. A city forbidding "busking" (in orderly fashion) on its pavements and squares must surely be the poorer for it, culturally. It is a tradition which probably descends from the time when minstrelsy was a source of the working-man's entertainment and continues to add life and character to an impersonal city-scape. Unless the stone hearts of modern cities are softened by the provision of pedestrian malls, street furniture and greenery, squares and pavement restaurants where people are encouraged to stop and interact, those cities will atrophy culturally.

Piazza Navone is a large rectangular space, closed to traffic, and boasts three fine fountains. The central fountain is known as the Fountain of the Four Rivers and each side portrays a world river – Nile, Ganges, Danube and Plate. We arrived at the right moment. It was sunset, street lamps in old fashioned "gas-lamp" design were beginning to glow softly, outdoor restaurants were filling up and the square seemed to sprout buskers. A man would appear carrying a folding table and chairs, set these up for business, and before long be reading a customer's palm or confidently foretelling his fortune based on the spread of the cards. Artists were setting up their easels for "instant" portraits or caricatures. Poster samples of the caricaturist's were on display: bulbous noses; jutting foreheads; long sagging chins; ears like radar dishes – no human feature exempt from acerbic exploitation by the masters of the grotesque. The silhouette artist would ask the customer to hold a steady profile while he, literally in seconds, provided an identical copy in black paper by the dexterous use of a pair of scissors, finally fixing the silhouette to a white backing card. Intricate detail: eyelashes; a stray wisp of hair; earrings and a good likeness ensured a satisfied customer. A gypsy lad of tender years played a small piano accordion while a kitten, connected to its master's leg by a string frolicked as only kittens know how. The musician's assistant, a young lady who had not seen her tenth birthday, did the rounds with an upturned hat.

We had been reminded before leaving home that big cities harbor, amid their broad sweep of citizenry, those souls whose calling it is to remove, unnoticed by their victim, the contents of bag or pocket. Rome is no exception.

In fact Rome is reputed to do rather well in this department. Of course the city got off to a bad start in 753 BC when Romulus slew his twin brother Remus in a dispute over the proposed boundaries of the new city. It had been my habit to warn the members of our party with a frequency and emphasis they found increasingly tedious, to be alert to this type of urban hazard – the pickpocket. On this evening we returned to the campsite in a crowded bus. "Beware pickpockets" I again cautioned. No seats were available and we were obliged to stand in the close throng. As the bus trundled along I became aware of my shoulder-bag seeming to "catch" on something several times. Instinctively I moved the bag to the other shoulder. Within seconds the "crowd" started pressing against me to the point of losing my balance. I now felt a plucking sensation in the region of my trouser pocket, upon which I turned savagely on a middle-aged, shifty-eyed man standing next to me. As I was now sure that my pocket/bag had been/was about to be picked I turned a ferocious face onto him. He was fortunate that the bus had stopped and he used this opportunity to alight with an alacrity which belied his years. I examined my bag to find the zipper fully open and passport and traveler's cheques partly dislodged, but intact. Needless to say I felt the full impact of my companions' sarcasm apropos "wakefulness against pickpockets".

The following day was devoted to a tour of Vatican City. This independent city-state would fit into a square of side measuring 660 metres, making it the smallest state in the world. The fact that the smallest state in the world contains the largest church in the world gives a clue to the raison d'etre of the Vatican. It is of course the spiritual font to Roman Catholics the world over. The Pope lives here as well as the governing body of the church, known as the Apostolic See. The Vatican City has all of 350 citizens, and a further 350 non-citizens also reside here. No practical distinction exists between the streets of the Vatican and the streets of Rome, and one moves between them without fuss. The Vatican City boasts well-stocked museums, including a charming room of statuettes and other objets d'art arranged by none other than Michelangelo. This artistic giant bequeathed to humanity his "La Pieta", a warmly moving expression of the pierced Jesus cradled in the Holy Mother's arms. The statue has been screened by vandal-proof glass since a hammer attack launched on it by a deranged man who was unable to participate in the joy of Pure Art. The famous vaulted ceiling of the Sistine Chapel (erected by Pope Sixtus the fourth in the 15th century) and the altar wall were decorated by Michelangelo and the power in these works is undiminished, as evidenced by the tens of thousands of visitors who come to pay homage each year. The scene on the wall depicts the "Last Judgment" while the ceiling shows nine scenes taken from the Old Testament entitled:

"Separation of Light and Darkness";
"Creation of Sun and Moon";
"Separation of Land and Water";
"Creation of Adam";
"Creation of Eve";
"Fall and Expulsion from Paradise";
"Sacrifice of Noah";
"The Great Flood";
"The Intoxication of Noah".

Painted nearly 400 years ago the colours are fresh and vital and have a pastel softness. The fourth scene, "Creation of Adam", is powerfully symbolical as God and Adam face each other with outstretched arms, index fingertips almost touching. The whole, including frescoes by other artists, is a visual and emotional banquet, too rich to be absorbed in one "sitting".

The focal point of the Vatican City is the Church of Saint Peter. Built originally over Peter's tomb, still preserved, the edifice has been extended over the centuries to become the splendid monument it is today. The lantern atop the dome (Michelangelo again) towers 120 metres above the floor of the church. The marble floor is marked out in the nave with the lengths of other world famous cathedrals including St.Paul's in London, all of which fall well short of St.Peter's. Richly decorated and lavishly ornamented one experiences a living museum.

We could not leave Rome without visiting the mysterious catacombs, that fertile ground where the seed of Christianity had been planted which would eventually engulf Rome, replacing paganism. The first Christians were driven underground, literally, by the authorities who rejected the notion of a self-proclaimed Saviour (he had caused some trouble previously in the Roman Province of Palestine) advocating the worship of a God who was not Jupiter.

The aggregate length of the underground passages comprising 80 catacombs runs to several hundred kilometers. Christian gatherings and services were conducted in rooms and chapels hewn from the soft bedrock. Large numbers of people, including the early popes, over succeeding centuries were buried along the subterranean galleries in shelf-like recesses cut one above the other in seemingly endless rows. As the conventional method of corpse disposal by the Romans was by cremation, it is probable that burial became necessary for Christian devotees due to the belief in future resurrection of the body. Frescoes decorating some crypts are in good condition.

Three days of city-life was long enough and we continued north up the west coast to the peninsula Monte Argenterio and the fishing village Porto San Stefano. Small boats crowded into a picturesque bay, and the fore-shore was lined with open-fronted shops where vendors enthusiastically, and vociferously, proclaimed the superior merits of their "fruits of the sea" – fresh fishes, squid, prawns, clams and mussels as well as some less identifiable items. After a stroll along the waterfront we found some open ground next to the sea where we could park the camper for the night. It was to be the night Peggy would remember as "the night of the tokoloshe" (African demon). It had turned stormy and rain lashed the windows. During a lull, Peggy was obliged to leave the camper for a few minutes. When she returned she noticed what appeared to be a wizened old man peering intently at our vehicle from a derelict shed nearby. Peggy's rest had now become a vigil – she swore later that she had even seen him move! Our suggestion in the morning that he must have been an Italian "tokoloshe" was not well received.

Continuing up the coast, we turned inland to visit Pisa. The town, situated on the river Arno, presented a patchwork-picture of earthy brick walls, red tiled roofs and sienna coloured dwellings which, as with many medieval towns scattered across Italy, has mercifully escaped the architectural excesses of modern urban planning. We were looking for the famous Leaning Tower but no street map was required as the tower soon poked up on the skyline. Leaning five degrees off the vertical, the tower is in no danger of toppling over until the centre of its mass moves beyond the limit of the base and subject to limiting ground support conditions. (There are moves afoot however to stabilize the structure). The tower was originally a campanile, or bell-tower, and it stands in the illustrious company of the duomo (cathedral) and baptistery. These three graceful structures dignify well-tended lawns. Their ornate architectural theme comprises closely spaced slender columns supporting arches, gables and domes constructed of white marble, giving the appearance of delicate filigree. We ran the gauntlet of souvenir booths bristling with monstrous plastic caricatures of the Tower, and jostled along with the Sunday crowd into the grounds.

The tower contains an internal stairway spiraling about a central core with doorways at each of the six levels giving access to the balconies. The narrow arched openings which comprise the façade of the tower are located at the outer edge of the balconies. No guard rails have been provided at the edge in order to preserve the aesthetic purity of the tower, and this tests visitors' nerves to the uttermost. As we ascended the stairway we emerged at each level to circumnavigate the balcony. Alternating in this way from a tilted helix to a tilted disc soon confused our "middle ear" and together with the unguarded balconies at the higher levels, imprinted material in our psyches for use in future nightmares. There were striking perspectives of duomo and baptistery from the summit of the tower as well as Pisa itself. We intended to reach Firenze (Florence) that afternoon, 85 kilometres further, so, back to the camper.

Entering from the west, one has a grand introduction to the beautiful wooded city of Florence from a view-site above the river Arno. We enjoyed the view at sunset in the company of a giant "David", tirelessly maintaining a vigil over the city, his sling to hand should a Goliath appear. This "David" is a four metre copy of Michelangelo's original sculpture housed in the Academy Gallery in the city below. A fragrance of the renaissance lingers over Florence. Art galleries abound; medieval squares and houses lie undisturbed; current exhibitions and concerts are advertised extensively. We noticed how the "feeling" of Italy changed in this province of Tuscany from the brash, undisciplined cities of Rome, Naples and points south, to an atmosphere more genteel and less hectic. This feeling would become more pronounced as we travelled north until it culminated in the "super-civilized" air of Switzerland. But this is running ahead.

We found a large well-appointed campsite. Here I had a brief encounter as trivial as it was embarrassing. Melody and I were strolling back to the camper having been to the camp shop. Believing myself to be in company with my daughter, I pointed to a cat crouching in a bush nearby and said in a mock falsetto: "Ooh look at the little pussy". Unbeknown to me however, Melody had dropped back on a private diversion and her place had been taken by an elderly, grizzled man of indeterminate nationality. As the remark was clearly aimed in his direction, the man felt obliged to glance at the cat, albeit somewhat disinterestedly. At the same instant I realized I had addressed the wrong "companion". There was nothing for it, I had to pretend to be a congenital idiot so I grinned lop-sidedly while rolling my eyes. I did feel my cheeks warming though.

Exploring the streets of Florence was very pleasant: the bell-tower (not leaning), cathedral and baptistery are works of art; Dante Alighieri's house is preserved as a monument; the Ponte Vecchio, so-called Old Bridge due to Etruscan foundations (c.400 BC), which spans the Arno bearing the iconic dwellings. This bridge was one of the few not destroyed by the German retreat during WWII. Possibly the best known art collection is held by the Uffizi Gallery, formerly the renaissance palace of Cosimo de Medici. He was the merchant-prince of that period of cultural "re-birth" and established an era of enlightenment and family dynasty which would rule Florence for 300 years. Cosimo also commissioned the young literary genius Marsilio Ficino to translate the Platonic Dialogues into Latin, thereby allowing Socrates to "speak" to those yearning for wisdom a millenium later.

One cannot adequately describe the wealth of paintings, sculptures and tapestries in the Uffizi Gallery. As with major galleries in other countries, the presentation of art works spanning many centuries is of such a range, variety and impact that discriminating viewing is essential to avoid "cultural indigestion". Unless one is art connoisseur or student with specialized interests and the opportunity for repeated visits, it is preferable to inspect part of the display unhurriedly than to attempt a more rapid viewing in the hope of not leaving anything out. The latter method is typified by the organized tour group. The leader brandishing catalogue or brolly like a standard-bearer in the van of a Roman Legion usually sweeps through museum or gallery pausing briefly at strategic points partly to give a hurried synopsis of an art-work, and partly to allow the main body of bemused "troops" to reach the front line, consolidate and sweep on in blitzkrieg fashion. Of course there was too much to appreciate at the Uffizi but we did our best.

We left Florence en route for the coast, and between Pistoia and Lucce called in at a small village called Collodi. Here was the birth-place and later became the pen-name of an author whose book would delight children (and their parents) for generations, and would be translated into every significant language in the world. The man: Carlo Collodi (real name Lorenzini); the story: Pinocchio. We wandered through Pinocchio Park where scenes from this allegorical work have been recreated in mosaics and bronze sculptures in a garden setting: Gepetto carving the wood; the inadvertent death of the cricket, later to appear as Pinocchio's conscience; the Fox and Cat at the Inn of the Red Crawfish; it was a delightful diversion. In these northern parts of Italy one does not travel far without seeing a medieval village perched on a hill-top. We visited one of these villages, having climbed several hundred metres above the surrounding plain, and drove in as far as the width of the road permitted, which was not very far. We parked in a small square which contained a statue of someone who meant something to the place (the patriot Garibaldi, I think) as well as an old fashioned water-pump. Unexpectedly, a number of teenage "punks" were nonchalantly draped around the fountain sporting the latest fashion in studded leather-ware. This contrasted with the background of centuries-old houses and cobbled streets. The houses did not seem unduly put out having witnessed many a strange sight in their long, stationery march through time and this too will disappear in the blink of a shutter. We ambled through the narrow cobbled ways, up or down a staircase, a sudden turn through a timbered archway, past a rose garden guarded by a cat pretending to be asleep. We strolled around the feudal castle at the summit and tried to decipher the trappings of a archeological "dig" nearby – its strung lines, numbered pegs and shallow pits revealing ancient crumbling masonry, indicating that someone was having a grand time with the past.

Back in the camper and the 20th century, we followed the Ligurian coastline, stopping for lunch on the road at the mountainside town of Portofino – stamping ground of the wealthy judging by the mansions overlooking the sea.

This is a pretty coastline with pastel coloured houses jumbled around compact bays stocked with fishing boats and yachts. The road carried us inland through forests until we reached Genoa, one of the oldest Mediterranean ports. The bustle of this large city encouraged us to keep moving and, 100 kilometres north of Genoa, we stretched our legs at the town of Tortona. Here a gigantic gilded statue of the Holy Virgin dominates the country-side from the steeple of a church. We pressed on to reach Milan before nightfall.

A dearth of campsites caused us to keep a lookout for a convenient place to park for the night, and we found what looked like a good one in farm-lands south of the city. The abundance of surrounding water: ditches, streams, bogs and canals should have warned us. We had no sooner chosen a quiet corner of a field when we were ambushed by clouds of mosquitoes. These girls (boy mosquitoes don't bite) attacked with an appetite voracious and a disregard for personal safety worthy of a kame-kazi pilot. Frenzied slapping preceded a rapid and ignominious retreat to pastures less "mosquitoed", and we ended up on the fore-court of a service station in a Milanese suburb. We awoke next morning well after the place had opened for business and the proprietor, with Italian graciousness, pretended not to notice the camper disgorging disheveled and strangely clad occupants, blinking in the sunlight. This was one of the few occasions that all five of us were obliged to sleep in the camper. We heaved the girls up onto their perch and put Mark on the front seat where he regularly informed us about its unsuitability for his 1,95 metre (6 foot 4) frame.

We had two main reasons for calling in at Milan. The first was to visit the famous cathedral. This is a magnificent work of art - a song of praise frozen in stone: architecturally lavish and yet harmonious in all its parts. A 14th century creation, the largest Gothic structure in Italy, is a reminder of what the human spirit is capable of when freed from the shackles of fear and superstition which preceded the renaissance. Over 4000 statues adorn the cathedral, within and without, and 135 spires add a touch of triumphal delicacy. We travelled to the roof using the lift in preference to a narrow claustrophobic-looking helical stair. The structure was undergoing full-scale restoration and a black "urban crust" up to 6 mm thick was being removed by grit-blasting. One could not help wondering whether fine detail of the embellishments was also disappearing. However the effect of the cleansed portions is vibrant. The creamy, honey tones of the stone spires and filigree decorating the roof buttresses, and fabric of the building generally, appears as a youthful complexion to the visage of the grand old lady. Within the cathedral are many fine carved and painted art- works and we reveled in the atmosphere created by 29 soaring columns lining each side of the nave.

Our second reason for calling in at Milan was to visit the refectory of the Church of Santa Maria della Grazie. Here in 1495, a genius from the small town of Vinci, midway between Pisa and Florence, together with his pupils created a work of art which must be one of the most special to reach us from the "age of enlightenment". The genius, Leonardo, was responsible for the huge mural stretching across the gable wall of the refectory – a magnificent scene depicting Jesus, in fellowship with his apostles, partaking of his Last Supper. This work exudes a powerful force of attraction. The eyes devour it and still come back for more. Jesus, the electric focus at the centre of the painting, is open-armed and wears an expression which is at once serene, compassionate and all-wise. The apostles are engaged in conversations, one of whom (is it John?) gazes at the Master with "supplicatory" eyes, and the whole is rich in expression and symbolism. This gem was almost reduced to rubble 448 years after its creation when the building suffered a direct hit from a bomb during an air-raid in 1943. Only the prior sand-bagging to both sides of the wall saved the painting from the international vandalism that is war.

As we would be passing Monza, near Milan, on our journey north, we decided to look in at the famous motor-racing circuit. Great was our excitement on finding that for a nominal sum we would be admitted to watch Formula 3 racing cars practicing for an event in a few days time. The track is in a beautiful setting of woods and parkland, the cherry trees were just fruiting and we had the pleasure (?) of hearing the air torn asunder by the high-pitched scream from finely tuned engines – a vivid contrast with the song birds that could be heard in the lulls and seemed not to mind the competition from the racers. Continuing northward we followed the eastern shore of Lake Como. The plains of Lombardy were becoming towering snow-capped mountains.

TO SWITZERLAND

June 24, Midsummer's Day: 3 months and 3 weeks since leaving Durban. We arrived at the Swiss border with the sense of excitement and anticipation that new borders always induced in us. We were almost two thirds through our European adventure; the camper was running like a Swiss watch - had carried us safely for 12 000 kilometres thus far, and miraculously, we were keeping to the planned budget of R 10 per person per day, personal pocket money excluded.

The transformation from Italy to Switzerland was obvious and immediate, despite the fact that northern Italians are calmer by nature than those folk living further south, where a more excitable "Mediterranean temperament" prevails. The bank where we changed our lire into Swiss francs, as well as the "Gasthof" (inn), both a stone's throw from the border post, was meticulously clean and wore a calm expression of controlled orderliness, a typical characteristic of the Swiss. For the next two weeks that we spent among the Alps in southern Switzerland we enjoyed an atmosphere of quiet relaxation: the absence of interests historical amply compensated by the abundance of wonders natural.

Within a few kilometres of the border we crossed the snow covered Maloja Pass, 1815 metres above sea level, and shortly after found a lovely campsite on a grassy meadow outside the ski resort of St. Moritz. If the first most outstanding feature of alpine countryside is the ever-present, white-capped, awesome, sharks' teeth skyline of the Alps, then the second most outstanding feature is the profusion of wild flowers. Peggy, in a transport of joy, would on occasion collect an armful without moving from one location.

The days were sunny and warm with the nights pleasantly cool. Near the campsite we discovered the bleached bones of a huge timber skeleton; naked in summer, but in winter clad in the cold white flesh of snow. This was the ski-jump, quietly hibernating. Mark and I climbed to the top to visualize the sensations of a ski-jumper. We decided the competitors would have to possess a strong suicidal tendency to step onto this slope, plummet downwards at a near frictionless high speed, be launched into the sky from the upturned lower end and soar gracefully until reaching the mountainside below.

This was the land of the "wandelpad" (walking path). Signage with Swiss precision informs hikers as to: destination, distance and walking duration. When we reached a sign that promised: "Silvaplana – 5 kilometres – 45 minutes", we accepted the invitation. A delightful stroll to the village led us through a wood here, past a small lake there, and at last to a cosy coffee shop, complete with tinkling bell attached to the front door, where we relished hot chocolate drinks and cream cake "snoep".

Later that evening we dined "al fresco" beside a lake near the campsite. On a distant bank we noticed a huge bonfire providing cheer to a number of young men who intermittently broke out into boisterous song. The boister increasing as the evening wore on, we suspected that they had been joined by the "genie" Bacchus, released from a bottle.

We had entered Switzerland as far east as was convenient with the intention of following the alpine range westwards. This entailed crossing the mountains via a series of spectacular passes and picturesque valleys, with streams and waterfalls to delight us at almost every turn. This is a land of abundant water and this is reflected in the lushness of the meadows.

From St. Moritz, we paused at the Julier Pass, 2284 metres, where we tobogganed down a snowy slope on our raincoats in a ridiculous and wildly hilarious fashion. At the summit we had sight of something which could not have been more out of keeping with the surroundings. In the cold and rarified air of the pass, we noticed a small green budgie fluttering unconcernedly along the edge of the escarpment, resting occasionally on a rocky outcrop. We briefly entertained the notion of catching the bird to "save" it from certain death by freezing, but it flew off while we gawped indecisively. Now the mountain road carried us down to the Via Mala Gorge where a river thundered through a giant cleft carved in the solid rock hundreds of metres deep – another wrinkle in the face of Mother Earth. The road rolled on through picture-postcard scenery:

cuckoo-clock houses trimmed with window-boxes cascading geraniums; fat white and tan cows with swollen udders and brass bells strapped to necks by broad leather collars, clonk – clonking through flower-rich pastures; farmers scything grassy fields for next winter's fodder; steepled churches in villages dozing beside swiftly flowing mountain rivers.

Seventy kilometers further to the Oberalp Pass (2044 metres), the other side of which lay our overnight stop at the village of Andermatt. Next day we faced the formidable Furka Pass (2431 metres) and after a slow crawl to the summit, we stretched our legs on a bleak and icy plateau where the mountain peaks had vanished in a swirling mist. A snow slope nearby lured us into several "raincoat" slides, again attended with jollity.

The mountain roads are engineering masterpieces as they loop back and forth on the steep mountainside gradients, each leg culminating in a tight hairpin bend requiring buses to use the full width of the road to negotiate. The scenery, a major distraction if one happens to be the driver, is breathtaking.

A few kilometres below Furka we were astonished to see a bright blue glow emanating from an icy hillside further down. This was totally inexplicable to us until we discovered the glow to be a glacier giving birth to a river: here was the source of the Rhone. This river, not to be confused with the Rhine further north, drains south-westwards to empty into the Mediterranean Sea, west of Marseille, France. Here, at its birthplace, a tunnel has been cut deep into the solid ice of the parent glacier at the end of which lies a cave. The semi-translucent walls gleamed with smooth wetness in the glare of the electric lamp, and it was odd to think of ourselves standing deep below the surface of this slowly creeping river of ice.

We now faced the final pass to our immediate objective, Interlaken. Although at 2164 metres not the highest, Grimsel Pass was by far the most impressive in its stark beauty. The road had been cleared of snow which had fallen in such vast quantities that huge sheer cliffs of "snow-packed-into-ice" lined the road, six metres high in places. The road appeared like an asphalt river snaking through an ice canyon. The snow-plough was still at work; nearby lay a small lake completely frozen over, and another partially. And this was mid-summer!

Our way descended slowly for 45 kilometres to Lake Brienz where an inflowing Rhine temporarily loses its identity. We followed the shore road to Interlaken, which as the name signifies, is situated between Lakes Brienz and Thun. This charming town is flanked by imposing hills to the north and the regal, and mysterious, Jungfrau Mountain to the south. The Jungfrau is likened to a shy "young maiden" due to infrequent glimpses of her when she parts her misty veil to reveal her majestic beauty. We would see her face at close-quarters a week later, but first – a campsite at Interlaken to be found.

We finally selected a site on the shore overlooking the Brienzersee paddle-steamer jetties. These large and colourful boats convey locals and tourists between lakeside villages. The swiftly flowing river on our "doorstep" looked cold as it raced through a narrow channel from Interlaken to Lake Thun. The crystal clarity of the water along the bank merged into turquoise opacity further from the shore, and resident ducks had their work cut out against the current. A pleasant five minute walk took us to the town where we rambled through the side streets inspecting the wooden double-storey houses, often decorated with carvings and flower-laden window boxes and hanging baskets. Many of the tiny, well-tended front gardens had a thriving vegetable patch.

On a late afternoon stroll to a neighbouring village, we searched out the source of muffled sounds of a brass band. Homing in, we finally stood before a quaint wooden building boasting a fret-worked sign which read "Muzikhaus". Through the window we saw a number of men "oompah-ing" on a variety of wind instruments. It was a treat to see and hear music made for the sheer joy of it. At an inn nearby we supped on ham rolls and coffee in a warm atmosphere of wood, leather and glinting copper.

Interlaken, although popular with tourists, has retained a "small village" character. The only jarring note is the modern multi-storey building set among red-tiled, pitched roofs of the indigenous architecture. The town is well situated for exploration of the surrounding district and picturesque lake-shore villages.

South of Interlaken, two valleys push into the Bernese Alps. Gluttons for the aesthetic purity of the mountains, we decided to spend time in each. At the terminus of the first valley we camped near the resort village of Grindelwald. The skyline to the south could hardly have been more spectacular. To the left: Schreckhorn; facing us, the brooding north face of the Eiger; to the right,

Sea facing cabin en route to Greece

Olympia, Greece - birthplace of the Games

Poseidon's temple at Cape Sounion, Greece

Girls peering into a smoking Vesuvius, Italy

Ice cave on Jungfraujoch, Switzerland

Glacier Chamonix, France

Camping Chamonix, France

Carcassonne medieval town, France

Gargoyle in Notre Dame Paris, France

Robin Hood Nottingham, England

Monch – these three giants tower four kilometres above sea level. A mysterious white light burned like a Cyclopean eye high up in Eiger's face during the dark hours, and little did we think that in three days we would be looking out over Grindelwald from that very spot on the sheer mountainside.

From the campsite we enjoyed several fine walks, including a long hike to the Obergletcher – the High Glacier. These refugees from the Ice Age (the glaciers) appear as a river of frozen waves and the surface becomes increasingly more ragged and spiky, with peaks and chasms, toward the end which is busy thawing into a living stream. Moving at a rate of a few centimetres a year, glaciers grind their way down mountain ravines imperceptibly.

We picnicked below the Obergletcher near signboards bearing dire warnings of danger; settled down to watch Mother Nature's cabaret and were not disappointed. At regular intervals a chunk of ice – anything from the size of a football to the size of a sofa – would part company from its parent with a loud crack and hurtle down a steep incline to shatter on rocks in the river bed. I fetched a piece that had landed nearby and we examined it closely. It was not a solid piece of ice as expected. Instead it comprised pea-sized crystals of clear ice which fragmented cleanly when given a sharp blow. We sucked the refreshing ice crystals and wondered if we were tasting ice-age water a few thousand years old. Delicious!

The contour path back led us through hill-sides garlanded with flowers; we also encountered farm life in the form of an inquisitive foal with "woolly" fur, his nonchalant mother and a gang of delightful kids, i.e. baby goats. On the day following we moved across to the other valley which radiates out from Interlaken.

This valley is quite different in character to the broad sweep of farmlands that nestled in the valley we were leaving. By contrast, here the mountainsides rise precipitously only 800 metres apart. The village of Lauterbrunnen (pure fountain) sprawls beneath a cliff and near a glacial waterfall, the highest in Europe, which plunges to earth in feathery spray. There are a number of glacial streams cascading over the escarpment further down the valley, and in a breeze they sway languorously to the silent rhythms of the air currents. The road into the valley ends at tiny Stechelberg, a clump of houses rather than village, and we camped on lush lawn next to a chattering stream.

The highlight of our stay was a journey up to the Jungfraujoch, a plateau situated between the Monch and the Jungfrau at an elevation of 2500 metres above Lauterbrunnen. We arrived at the mountain-railway station exhaling puffs of crisp morning breath, exuding excited anticipation and hoping fervently for clear weather up on the roof of the world. The train hauled itself up the steep gradient out of the valley on its cogs and we watched the town sink out of sight from the warmed coach. Soon we were above the tree line and encountering the "white stuff". The train stopped briefly at the ski resorts of Wengen and Kleine Scheidegg, and again at the stop "Eigergletcher", before entering the most remarkable section of the two hour journey. At this point, somewhere near the base of the Eiger's north face and about 1650 metres below the summit, the railway track plunges into the bowels of the mountain. An absolute marvel of engineering, the tunnel passes close to the Eiger's face, and from a station a gallery has been driven to the face itself. From here one looks out upon the Grindelwald valley thousands of metres below. This explained the mysterious light we had seen in the sheer face of the Eiger from the campsite. The tunnel now doubles back, climbing all the while, and we burrow deeply into the skeleton of our planet from the Eiger to the Monch, although from the inside there is nothing to distinguish the one from the other. The tunnel finally emerges at the Jungfraujoch, a vast snowfield in the lap of the Young Maiden. From the terminus, we passengers passed along an enclosed covered-way with frequent and large windows against the exterior of which snow had banked up. This gave the impression of shop windows displaying the merchandise available within (or more accurately, without).

We emerged to find a bright sun (it lacked warmth) and bracing air. Our pre-packed breakfast we enjoyed "al fresco", and crunched delightedly about on the virgin "white stuff" in our plastic boots. Apart from the occasional rocky spurs, all was softly rounded in white. At the top of an embankment the wind had formed a wafer-thin lace-edged crust of ice – it was delicious! Before long we discovered the Ice Palace: a network of passages and alcoves cut into the underlying glacier. A thermometer informed that it was -3 deg. Celsius. A car, large enough to sit in, had been carved from ice in one of the niches and had been impressively illuminated. Other diversions available were visits to a scientific museum and a weather station, but the fun of the afternoon lay at the summer ski school.

We hired skis which included five minutes of ski tuition, but learning was to be largely empirical. Initially, we were entertained by a crop of novices receiving their five minute "basic training" and later dutifully entertained others when our turn arrived. None of our party had ski-ed before and we were in good company judging by screams and flailing limbs all around. The fundamental concept that skis will move, seemingly of their own accord, unless positioned horizontally on the snow contour, is of paramount importance to control and stability. The penalty Nature exacts if this is forgotten, or not understood, is felt immediately. The feet become independent entities, each with its own private destination, and they endeavour to split the owner's torso; or rotate ankle, knee or hip joints, singly or in combination, into postures foreign to laws of human physiology. Having slithered down the "practice" slope, it became obvious that short of removing one's skis and tramping laboriously (and ignominiously) back up, one had to do some fast learning to reap the benefit of the ski-lift provided. This initially took the form of watching others engage with the lift, certain that one would not be quite as useless as some of the less proficient folk were demonstrating – only to be proved wrong of course. The mechanics of the lift were quite simple in principle and comprised an endless steel cable continuously running through large horizontally secured sheave wheels at the lower and upper ends of the slope. Fixed to the waist-high cable at regular intervals, and at right angles to the cable, were wooden handles about 30 cm long. Shod with skis, one positioned oneself facing the uphill slope alongside the cable and in a moment of confidence (desperation?) lunged at the next handle to arrive. In theory, one would be immediately whisked from zero velocity to about 10 kilometres per hour within a few arm-stretching seconds, to be drawn effortlessly up the slope. In practice, in the space of a few heart-stopping seconds, one is often to be found sprawled on the snow. Although ski lift users discovered original ways of making fools of themselves, there were a few standard recipes for courting disaster: one foot heads east while the other heads west; both feet on a correct heading except that somehow they accelerate to a speed several kph faster than the rest of the body; alternatively, the feet take on a leaden quality thereby transforming this wonderful labour-saving device into a modern-day medieval rack with feet and hands gradually drifting apart. However, folks subjecting themselves to such various indignities did so in a good spirit – and there were many cases of the hopeless aiding the helpless.

All afternoon the sun blazed out of a cloudless sky and after three hours of ski-ing/falling we'd had enough. While we were resting, a strange feeling of nausea crept through our bodies. We had clearly overdone things in the rarified atmosphere 3454 metres above sea level. The signs we had noticed hitherto but failed to appreciate became clear: "Walk! Do not run". We were suffering a mild attack of oxygen-deprivation. And that was not all! The faces of our party, with the exception of yours truly whose face was protected by its hirsuteness, were glowing like beacons on a dark night. For the next few days they would suffer the effects of radiation burns from the snow-reflected sunlight on that memorable afternoon. In time, their dolorous expressions disappeared as their blistered faces crumbled away revealing shiny new pink ones, like so many rare butterflies emerging from their chrysalises. There is an excellent restaurant in this alpine wonderland and we enjoyed hot chocolate while waiting for the last train of the day leaving at 6 pm. The Swiss, not content with providing a facility whereby folk in summer dress and ordinary shoes may safely and speedily be transported into a mountain fastness which not long ago was the preserve of well-equipped, experienced mountaineers only, are intending to drive the tunnel onward and upward from the Jungfraujoch with the object of breaching the maidenhead of the Young Maiden herself and establishing a terminus on the summit.

The next day, having bid farewell to enchanting Lauterbrunnen, we meandered along the Simmental (Simmen-valley). We looked in at Gstaad out of curiosity, and found a bustling village dressed in bunting and sporting a crop of elegant-looking tourists patronizing elegant-looking shops. We stopped overnight at a mediocre campsite at the eastern end of Lac Leman (Lake Geneva), a huge stretch of water shaped like a fat banana with Geneva lying at the western end. The influence in this region of Switzerland is French and the previously high-gabled houses become rather box-like. As we moved south towards the frontier at Vallorcine, the profusion of wild flowers in the meadows again drew the ladies out of the camper to "go-a-gatherin'".

TO FRANCE

At the border-post French red-tape had us filling in forms even though our visas were valid. A gendarme asked Peggy: "Parlez vous Francaise?" No, she replied. "Un deficiencie!" retorted the policeman, which required no translation. At this Peggy, stiffly said: "But I can speak Zulu!" and stumped out of the office leaving a rather bemused officer. This minor incident illustrated the disdain of the French towards anyone "unfortunate" enough not to be French. This unfriendly attitude, however, is more than compensated by the beauty of their country. Nowhere is this more dramatically evident than in the valley down which we were driving towards the resort town of Chamonix. To our left, glaciers were spilling out of ravines like whipped cream. The huge dome of Mont Blanc, 4800 metres above sea level, stands sentinel over Chamonix, and under its gaze we found a grassy field in which to camp. This was an annexe to a campsite filled to capacity, and we settled in for the following two days. As we explored the surroundings it became plain that Chamonix was a "hot-bed" for outdoor enthusiasts. Rock-faces swarmed with youngsters roped together, and on a visit to a glacier, there they were – popping in and out of ice-crevasses, or climbing sheer ice faces, driving hand-picks hand over hand into the icy surface as they tip-toed up the face in boots looking like porcupines; or hiking; or cycling; or fishing; look up and you may see a glider or hang-glider soaring in the up-draughts.

The charming town of Chamonix has a river chattering purposefully through its length. We could not leave without taking a chair-lift several hundred metres up a hillside, swinging over the tree tops in leisurely fashion. At the upper station we were able to partly inspect a glacier at close quarters. Far removed are glaciers from the frozen inert mass that they appear from a distance. Along the edges the frictional thaw ensures constant activity as ice and earth coalesce into mud and slush. The glacier's surface is ragged and uneven and crevassed. One of the larger glaciers, the "Mer de Glace" (Sea of Ice), races down its ravine bed at a breathtaking 3 mm per hour.

Another attraction, one that the ladies preferred to watch rather than use, was a dry toboggan run that Mark and I ventured to try. The toboggan, a wheeled wagon just large enough to sit on, ran within a dish-shaped concrete channel. This channel winds down the hillside in varying gradients for about a kilometre. Speed in the toboggan is controlled by braking with a "joy-stick" which if not tugged, lets gravity "get on with it". A leaflet claimed a record speed of 30 kph had been achieved and hunkered in the channel, streaking down the straights and rearing up on the banked turns, it felt more like 100 kph!

Our intention was now to head down to the French Riviera, but being close to Geneva thought it a good opportunity to visit this city.

BACK TO SWITZERLAND

At 7 pm that evening we re-entered Switzerland and had managed to squeeze into a campsite on the bank of the Lake. Geneva has a clinical orderliness about it – a legacy of John Calvin perhaps. He was the 16th century religious reformer who restored moral integrity to a corrupt town by banning such pleasures as dancing and similar frivolities, and espousing the moral tonics of hard work and fair dealings. The large buildings housing bureaux subordinate to the United Nations such as International Labour, World Health, and so on, lend those parts of the city a sober, almost pompous, air of efficiency. The real charm of the city however, lies in the old quarter where antique and book shops line the cobbled streets, overlooked by 19th century gas lamps. Pleasure in the city has obviously been "unbanned". Festivities were being held along the shore of the lake and colourful marquis tents were there in numbers to satisfy the "inner man and woman". Nearby a crowd of youngsters on roller-skates were entertaining passersby with impromptu slalom races round a line of soft drink cans, and ramp-jumps over a bar set chest-high. At the end of a jetty projecting into the lake stands the iconic urban symbol of the city – a solitary high-pressure jet of water surging powerfully to a height of 150 metres. This super-fountain seems to typify the Swiss psyche: clean; crisp; purposeful; direct.

Later we enjoyed a swim from the campsite's private beach on a "day off" spent lazing in the sun, and watched the yachts idly frolicking in the breeze. The 80 kilometre long lake drains through the city centre, the canalized water shoving powerfully as if anxious to resume its identity as the Rhone, having been pent up quite long enough in the lake.

BACK TO FRANCE

We said goodbye to Switzerland and headed south, en route for the coast. At Grenoble we chose the Route Napoleon, for no other reason than the vaguely romantic connotation carried by the name. We were travelling in the opposite direction taken by Napoleon Bonaparte when he secretly returned to France in 1815 having escaped from the island-prison of Elba. (Had Napoleon been an English speaker he might well have used the palindromic expression: "Able was I ere I saw Elba").

The reign of Louis 18th was threatened by Napoleon's return, so he dispatched his troops with orders to dispatch Napoleon. Story has it that when the troops intercepted Napoleon and his supporters at Grenoble, the ex-emperor, recognized many soldiers who had served under him, seized the initiative and leapt from his horse, threw open his cloak and cried: "If there is one amongst you who wishes to kill his emperor, let him come forward and do so, here I am!" The tension, which must have been electric, was eventually broken by one of the men who called out: "Long live the Emperor!" Thereupon the troops switched their allegiance and Napoleon carried on triumphantly to Paris. He might have saved himself the trouble as only a few months later he would meet his Waterloo. This time the island-prison chosen for him lay deep in the South Atlantic at St.Helena. The commemoration of his journey from the coast is an equestrian statue of the great man by the roadside.

Our overnight stop was at a small and charming village by name of Chauffayer. Here, as well as elsewhere in France, ablution facilities are adequate, although French "laissez aller" permits the communal use of facilities by both male and female. It took all of seven minutes to stroll the length of the village main street that evening under the dim glow of a sprinkling of electric lamps.

Amid the gentle breath of the sleeping village, the bakery advertised its vital function by exhaling a delicious aroma of fresh baking out into the night air. Outside an old and faded double-storey villa we were briefly held in our ramble by the enchantment of a piano being played within – the twinkling notes drifting into the embracing silence.

Next morning, strike camp and back to the Route Napoleon. Attractive scenery passed by our windows – mountains, rivers, a rocky gorge, until we turned off for Nice via the old perfume town of Grasse. Here thousands of tons of flowers are processed every year in order to yield those subtle essences which have established the reputation of French perfumes. A delicate but unmistakable sweetness hangs in the air over Grasse.

As streams feed rivers which fatten as they approach the sea, so did the road tributaries fill with an increasing volume of traffic the roads leading to the sea at the French Riviera, but unlike a river which discharges its load into the sea, the roads become increasingly choked by the summer tide of vehicles. The northern shore of the Mediterranean Sea attracts hundreds of thousands of: sun-seekers; wind-surfers; hikers; campers; caravaners; beach goers; and holiday makers from points north, all of whom seek a share of the summer sunshine.

We crept at snail-pace through Nice and Monte Carlo (a convenient speed for sight-seeing) looking for a campsite. Due to the mountainous nature of the area usable land is at a premium and given the popularity of the Cote d'Azur, it is not surprising that land-hungry campgrounds are scarce. Having been turned away from several fully booked sites we at last managed to squeeze into a small site in Menton at the foot of a medieval village called Gorbio. The cobbled ways in this charming village could be spanned with outstretched arms and the two-storey houses seem to lean tiredly towards each other in their dotage. In the campsite we found an adjacent apricot orchard (fruit trees in campsites being "fair game") and proceeded to cram the fruit into pockets until we were distracted by urgent yells from a nearby house – it seems the orchard was not in the campsite after all!

For the next few days we worked our way westward along the Riviera. First call: Monte Carlo. Residents in the mini-state of Monaco, of which Monte Carlo is the principal city, do not pay personal income tax – the state generating much of its income from the famous casino. This ornately decorated and turreted building looks more like a royal palace than the Royal Palace itself. Elegantly attired doormen sneer superciliously down Gallic noses at tourists gawping in at the glass doors. During the daytime at this high-class gambling den visitors are admitted, appropriately dressed and over 18 years of age, to lighten their wallets in the plush, maroon "one-arm bandit" rooms. Indeed we sustained the life of the State for one or two milliseconds by losing a few rands. These avaricious machines are so unsatisfying in terms of entertainment value that habitués of the sport find themselves spooning in coins and jerking the operating handle in a continuous glassy-eyed rhythm to ameliorate the frustration at their lack of success. In the foyer of the building we viewed an excellent display of the extravagant couture of a bygone age.

We mistimed our visit to the royal palace by arriving a few minutes after the changing of the guard. The new guards, immaculately turned out in white uniforms and pith helmets, were stationed in front of guard-boxes painted in "barber-pole" red and white diagonal stripes, which lent more of a carnival than martial spirit to the scene. Our ladies' disappointment at missing the guards' changing was lifted by a glimpse of the princess Stephanie who emerged from the palace in a large black limousine which roared away at speed. We enjoyed the fine view of Monte Carlo and its boat-speckled harbor from the palace precincts which are situated on an elevated promontory.

Later, we visited the mountain-top village of Eze from which, again, there were magnificent views of the coastline: the occasional motor launch trailing a white comet-like tail against an azure background; the sea itself fading into a sheet of silver as it stretched to the horizon. Eze has the peculiarity of having to bury the bodies of its departed above, instead of below, ground level. This is due to the difficulty of excavating into solid bedrock and most "graves" in the tiny cemetery are sarcophagi. Leaving the dizzy heights of Eze we drove through Nice, with its beach frontage of grandiose, but slightly seedy-looking, hotels, along a palm-lined boulevard and so onto the coastal road. Passing through Antibes, and Juan les Pins we found a campsite at Cannes. The late afternoon was warm and humid and the beach beckoned. Typically for this stretch of coastline, wind surfers and bathers are out in force. Males and females generally displayed uniformity in choice of swimwear, that is, bottoms only. Peggy and the girls felt somewhat outraged by this obvious breach of feminine modesty which, by association, seemed to betray the refinement of womankind, and naturally Mark and I had to agree, being outnumbered.

The following day was Bastille Day, July 14, France's Independence Day. In the campsite we observed a party of young children celebrating by way of a rather bizarre game. A line was strung from which was suspended a number of water-filled balloons. A short distance away the participants were, by turns, blindfolded, spun round several times and pointed in the direction of the balloons. The "sightless" child was armed with a long stick from which a nail projected at the remote end. At a signal, the child stumbled towards the targets to the raucous accompaniment of advice from spectators: "Arretez"; "a' Droite"; "a' Gauche"; "Avancez", with the effect of completely confusing the striker. He swung his stick in the direction he guessed the balloons to be, and if successful created a great splash as the balloon exploded, followed by a general cheer from bystanders. Those who futilely flailed fresh air earned scorn from their peers. What was the significance of this game I wondered? The head-like symbolism of the balloon, from which gushed liquid contents after a violent blow: a simple child's game?...or a re-enactment of the grisly events at the Bastille in Paris on 17 July 1789, which climaxed with the Governor's head carried about the streets on the end of a pike?

Having a "last-look" round the harbor at Cannes, we were struck by the aura of affluence engendered by the great white motor-yachts with shining brass bells and scrubbed decks and huge floral bouquets tastefully placed on the after-decks. A ferry was about to depart for the nearby island of St.Marguerite and we jumped at this new opportunity. This non-commercialized wooded isle, which may be circumnavigated in an hour's striding, has as its principal edifice a centuries-old fortress that today provides dormitory accommodation for youth groups. The castellated tower and bastions; the sea breeze snapping the stiffly extended "tricolor"; the ochre plaster crumbling off the walls; the dusty parade ground shimmering under a fierce sun; all the ingredients for visualizing the tough life of a Foreign Legion outpost were here. A certain prison cell in the fortress was the scene of "real-life" drama in the dark years of 18th century political intrigue. It was here that the legendary "man in the iron mask" was imprisoned and whose identity has ever since been a matter of conjecture. Was he too important, or noble, to be executed? Why save the man yet kill his identity? Why was a tightly fitting metal helmet riveted permanently over his head? Three sets of iron bars fragment the sky beyond the small window of his cell, and the grimy walls bear sooty scratches and half-faded graffiti which tell of years of dismal hopelessness. We leisurely explored the little island: a reedy "marais" (marsh) populated by sea birds and surrounded by bracken; and further on, a pine wood providing welcome coolth. Too soon was it time for the ferry back to the mainland, the camper and the long road once more.

The coastline along the Riviera is surprisingly rugged and relatively undeveloped, with red cliffs towering over secluded coves and inlets; or alternatively with the softer textures of pine forests sweeping down to the water's edge. This excellent marine drive is interspersed by delightful villages: Le Trayes, Agay, St.Raphael, providing visions of sleek yachts and colourful fishing boats in cosy havens, pretty houses, a turquoise sea. We camped near St.Tropez which we found to be a charming place. Two, three and four storey houses of earthy pastel shades face a small harbor with yachts and stone-cobbled quays. The artists' easels set up at various points showed that other eyes were also appreciating. A calm sea and balmy weather lured us into the water at a popular beach known as Tahiti, a few kilometers south of St.Tropez. The beach itself was curiously divided into screened areas, each advertising itself as belonging to a certain club. Acres of gently browning flesh lay distributed across the sands while the ubiquitous wind-surfers were hard at work.

We had reached the end of the stretch of coast known as the Cote d'Azur and now headed for Marseille. An exploratory diversion this side of Marseille paid off. We found the Calanques, a place as grandly impressive as it was unexpected. A sheer-sided ravine at least thirty metres deep and a thousand long, sliced through rocky hills to open out into the sea. That this inlet was a perfect anchorage was borne out by two rows of yachts moored in line abeam for hundreds of metres. This vast profusion of boats confirmed the popularity of Mediterranean cruising. Was there anyone living in these parts who did not own a yacht? The region was incongruously undeveloped, even "wild". No affluent yacht club or information centre was present, not even a decent road for that matter. A group of young hikers passed by toting packs and water canisters and manifested the enthusiasm of "Youth on an Adventure" with every bouncing step. Lying among derelict machinery were several children's jerseys, clearly abandoned but in reasonable condition. Peggy was at that moment presented with a mental image of shivering black babies back home in South Africa, and she felt she could not in all conscience turn her back on those jerseys. (A long while later, she had the pleasure of handing them to a beaming black woman on a dusty farm road near Richmond in Natal).

The quality of light in the Marseille environment is noticeably different, possibly as a result of the reflection of sunlight off the large areas of pale rock formations characteristic of the region. The effect is that colours appear in softer, warmer tones. The charm of Marseilles lies mainly in the Vieux Port (Old Port) and the surrounding old quarter. The main street leading away from the old port, the Canebiere, is a-bustle with market stalls. American tourists have paraphrased the name of this street as "can o' beer" in their inimitable way. Greek and Roman foundations have been excavated in the city confirming the history book information that Marseilles was founded by the Greeks (in 600 BC). Ever since those days the city has been a principal port and gateway into the hinterland. Near the Old Port stands a French Foreign Legion base and we stood at the gates peering into the grounds. I guess we half expected/hoped to see a thick set German drill sergeant sadistically double-marching a platoon of "legionnaires-of-all-nationalities-fleeing-justice", the hot dust rising from scuffing boots searing their parched throats. A soldier on guard-duty stared dully at us.

Further along, the road becomes the Promenade de la Corniche, a marine drive with attractive views to a sprinkling of islands, one of which is the fortified island of If. (On this island is the Chateau d'If which features in Alexander Dumas's novel "The Count of Monte Cristo"). Still further along the Corniche one finds the Champ de Courses, the horse racing track; and on this day we caught a glimpse of sulky-racing. The horses seemed to float by as they drew the incredibly frail-looking sulkies in a flowing, rhythmical gait which appeared almost leisurely in contrast with the headlong gallop of a race-horse.

From Marseilles it was not a long run to Arles. This old town has a Roman amphitheatre around which the medieval quarter was developed. Here, as in other historical settings one frequently comes across in Europe, one senses the imperceptible, almost static, passage of time. Towns and cities and their contents are really the artifacts of their inhabitants, and where these have been preserved provide a direct link with the past. The bones of these artifacts, being of baked clay, cement, beaten metal, carved stone and wood: endure longer than the bones of their makers and thus by proxy we can connect with our fore-bears.

In Arles we met up again with the river Rhone, now heavy and sluggish, first seen as a blue glow in a glacier on the other side of Interlaken. We sought out the house of Vincent van Goch who lived his final tragic years in Arles, only to discover that his neighbourhood had been a victim of aerial bombardment during the last war (international vandalism again). The area presently comprises traffic islands. What has endured however, apart from his memory and his work, is one of the charming subjects of his paintings: "The Bridge at Arles" (1888). No longer in use and declared a national monument, the little drawbridge stands serenely in a "drawn" position (in salute to the master?), the hardwood beams and posts and bold cross-bracing slowly becoming bleached by the sun. Two pretty "mademoiselles" were busy sketching the bridge – thereby somehow forging a link with Vincent beyond Time and Death.

We followed the east bank of the Rhone into the extraordinary region known as the Camargue. A 400 square kilometre reserve alongside the sea, the Camargue comprises numerous islets, lagoons and marshes, as well as grassy prairie inhabited by herds of untamed white horses and, oddly, black bulls. To reach the Camargue proper we had to cross to the west bank of the Rhone, achieved by means of a pontoon ferry across several hundred metres of swirling river. Flamingoes and sea birds occupied the reedy shallows of the "marais"- it was a privilege to take a slow drive through this beautiful and unspoiled region.

At Narbonne, another old Roman town, we stopped for lunch on a river bank where broad, mellowing stone steps led to the water's edge. Large heavy iron rings built into the quay wall suggested a time when rivers were significant commercial "highways". Nearby there stood an unfinished cathedral boasting the longest clear span Gothic arch in Europe.

Driving inland on a 56 km excursion, we arrived at Carcassonne, a settlement that has been fortified since its foundation by the Roman Julia Carcaso in 40 BC. Carcassonne is steeped in a history of military occupation: from Roman times to the Barbarian and Visigoth invasions of the 3rd and 4th centuries; to the 7th when occupied by Arab Saracens; thereafter to the various aristocratic power struggles leading to the Pope's 12th century crusade against the Cathars, a puritanical splinter off the Church in 1229. As the centuries crawled by, from the 13th to the middle of the 19th when restoration commenced, as the guide book tells us, Carcassonne fell into a deep slumber within its armoured façade. The result: a medieval town that has remained unchanged for 700 years. It has been suggested that among the various French architectural styles three distinct pinnacles have emerged. Secular: represented by the buildings of Mont St. Michel on the Norman coast; Ecclesiastical: by the cathedral at Chartres; Military: by Carcassonne. The complex attained classical perfection when Philip the Bold completed the works in 1285. Our first clear sight of the town was from a low knoll some distance away, and we were not prepared for what we found.

Situated on high ground in the plain of Languedoc, the castellated ramparts, punctuated by barbicans and towers, protectively ensconce the ancient town of Carcassonne. We stared, almost disbelieving our eyes, at this vision of the past: a sight that must have greeted many a traveler – or invader. In pre-artillery days, the town was virtually impregnable and conquest would have been possible only by siege or treachery. Two high walls encircle the town and the twenty metre distance between them is known as the "Lice" (the Lists). Regularly spaced along the walls, both inner and outer, are defensive towers with their distinctive conical black or red roofs. The towers flanking the main gates were constructed with V-shaped vertical projections to deflect missiles and loopholes with chamfered edges gave archers a wide field of vision should the outer wall be breached. If this did occur, the attackers would find no refuge in the captured outer towers as these were left open in their rear so that defenders could fire into them from the inner wall positions. The resident Duke was further protected by a moated castle within the town. Atop his ramparts were "hourdis", or overhanging timber galleries from which could be dropped rocks and hot liquids. The lower portion of the walls below the hourdis slope outwards to deflect these missiles towards the enemy. In the town is an impressive 12th century chateau and the charming cathedral of St. Nazaire. We spent a few delightful hours exploring the maze of cobbled streets among quaint houses of that distant period.

We now turned to Perpignan where Mark had yet to acquire a Spanish visa if we were to proceed further south. It was time to take stock and review our plans. We had been travelling for twenty weeks and had six remaining. The camper was purring along, using a little oil. We had added 16 000 kilometres to the odometer since March 3. We were enjoying the best of health and had lost our city "flab" and felt well-tuned and alert. The dynamic gypsy lifestyle we were experiencing was proving to be a great tonic, not only for the physique but for the psyche as well.

Spain lay before us with Portugal beyond.

There also remained France to the north: the Loire, Brittany, Paris…. and England also, were waiting to be explored. It was clear that time-effective planning was becoming essential as the tyrant Time was now exerting his authority.

TO SPAIN

Well, Spain it would be – at least some of it anyway. We crossed the border at Port Bou and followed the rugged coastline of Catalonia: the "Costa Brava" (wild coast) aptly named with cliffs and headlands, coves and rocky promontories to a backdrop of a blue, blue sea fringed with white foam along the shore. After stopping for lunch at the charming harbor village of Cadaques, we pressed on to Tossa del Mar where we would spend the night. This popular holiday resort provided a smart campsite: illuminated swimming pool; sports pitches; shop and restaurant and clean ablution blocks. We would see another luxurious campground such as this at Barcelona which illustrated the importance that was being attached to camping comforts for the tourist trade. These sites were fairly expensive (R 12 per night for the five of us). After an evening swim in the camp pool, we treated ourselves to bacon and eggs and sangria at the restaurant while we pondered on the possible interpretations of the sign which read: "Charge your roasted chicken". Wine is good value for money in Spain, but not always gentle on the palate. Sangria, however, is a red wine in which fruit chunks have been steeped, slightly tart yet sweet, like a fruit punch. In any case whatever it was, the result was that our carafe' required refilling a few times that evening. On returning to the camper, which I had parked in an open area suspiciously devoid of other campers, we discovered that we had become the target of an ant invasion. In an attempt to colonize the camper an unbroken column of black-ants was intrepidly scaling the rubbery slope of one of the tyres followed by a purposeful march into the grocery cupboard. The eggs they carried with them indicated the intention of a prolonged sojourn; possibly with the idea of abandoning the mother-planet in the hope of migration to a new ant galaxy by way of this great metallic spacecraft. It was a well disciplined contingent that had settled into cracks and crevices of their choice. Not so the renegade band that found their way into the girls' pup tent keeping them awake for hours as thousands of tiny feet clambered about leaving no body unturned in their search for food/shelter/comfort. This adventurous colony was our uninvited travelling companion for the next three weeks before we finally saw the last of it. Before leaving Tossa the next day, we explored the narrow streets of the "old town" which has retained many of the centuries-old defensive walls. On a rising promontory, fortifications with a circular watch-tower protectively overlook a little harbor.

We reached Barcelona at about four that afternoon having followed the coastal road from Tossa. The anxiety which occasionally arose when entering a large city without a street map was forestalled here as a result of a prominently situated tourist information office (open thankfully) on the main road. Staffed by students who seemed to be enjoying their work, we received a "kit" containing city map and other brochures. Tremendous urban development has taken place in Barcelona in the 20th century resulting in the creation of a regular grid of city blocks measuring 100 x 100 metres. Whilst lacking in creative town-planning, the system allows for simplified direction finding and smooth traffic flow. The Gothic quarter near the sea-front is largely unchanged, and as the port has a long history of human settlement, ancient Greek and Roman foundations, as well as artifacts pre-dating these, are being uncovered by archeological "digs" where new buildings are to be erected.

At a campsite just beyond the city limits we were offered a choice of camping "naturally" or "normally". I had till then thought it was natural to be normal, but here it appeared that it was natural to be naked. We chose to remain unnatural, but in any case sought another site with a less exorbitant tariff. We eventually found a spacious and well-wooded campground that advertised its presence by a billboard bearing the picture of a bright-eyed whale. At the entrance boom we were met by a uniformed attendant wearing a holster complete with revolver. With the site securely fenced we wondered what kind of undesirable entity prowled the precinct that required resistance by force of arms. We never found out who required shooting, but, along with fellow campers, encountered undesirables of a different kind. Shortly after sunset the camp was besieged by hordes of audacious mosquitoes determined to feed on human blood, even at the cost of their lives. A staccato of defensive slapping rose into the air until the camp management, in what seemed to be a routine operation, counter-attacked in a mechanized "blitzkrieg". A tractor drawing a machine with a 15 centimetre barrel that belched a thick cloud of black smoke of indeterminate toxicity made its way through the grounds. Soon the sounds of slapping were replaced by choruses of coughing, but at least the battle had been won.

Up early next morning to see new things in the city. We spent an hour or so at the Military Museum housed in the fortress Montjuich overlooking the harbor. Battle scenes of Imperial Spain were displayed along with uniforms, armour and weapons. (I looked for but could not find reference to the Armada of Drake's day). Our guide was a helpful youth who said he welcomed every opportunity to practice his English. Modern weaponry was also on display but did not have the fascination afforded by those relics of the Conquistadores and the Spanish Main; and the adventurers: Columbus; Cortez; Bilboa. Gold, stolen from the New World, gave rise to generations of pirates, and "privateers" who were "private" pirates whose country of origin sanctioned acts of piracy against their enemy fleets. There were mementos from the Arabian Conquest – the Islamic invaders from Africa whom the Spanish named the Moors – long-barreled rifles with characteristically flared butt, inlaid with ivory, and wicked looking curved scimitars decorated with semi-precious stones. Until their expulsion from Spain in 1491, the Moors had occupied most of the Iberian Peninsula.

Not far from the fortress, towards the city, lies a village named "Pablo Espanyol" which means Spanish Village. This "village" is a delightful exhibition of Spanish architectural styles, portrayed by eighty buildings grouped according to geographical regions of Old Spain. Enlivening the village were a number of craft and cottage industries in action. Visitors could observe the traditional activities of: glass-blowing; metal and leather work; wood-carving; ceramics; embroidery; all in simulated authentic surroundings. We had tantalizing glimpses of cobbled alleys angling off between quaint houses that were often decorated with flower-boxes cascading geraniums or bougainvillea; and photogenic scenes framed by a parade of tiled arches; here an intimate "plaza" (square); there an entrance leading into a garden courtyard with flower pots attached to white-washed walls, a burbling fountain in one corner and a welcome bench to relax weary feet and simply enjoy. The creators of this well-conceived village have indeed managed to capture a sense of the tranquil pace of life of yester-century when the ruling passions were other than Rush and Hurry.

We drove to town and parked the camper near the Parque de la Ciutadella (public gardens) intending to spend the rest of the day on foot, the only way to really see anything. Little did we imagine as we strolled away that High Drama would be awaiting our return some ten hours later – but more of that anon. We made our way to the Monumental Bull Fight Stadium to visit the museum on the premises. There was no fight scheduled for that day but, no matter, none of us were keen to witness a bull-fight anyway. The stadium has a high brick façade penetrated by tall, narrow arched openings, capped by a frieze of blue and white patterned ceramic tiles. The corners of the building are surmounted by large egg-shaped domes, tiled in the style of the frieze. At pavement level, two metre high posters advertise forthcoming events with colourful depictions of Fearless Matadors dealing decisively with their Tauran adversaries, always black. Within the stadium, tiers of seating expand concentrically outwards above a circular arena. The silent and empty amphitheatre, the neatly raked disc of sand, gave the impression of a bizarre temple awaiting the next service when another ritual sacrifice will stain the sandy altar with living blood. In the continued popularity of a "sport" pitting man against beast in an age where ecology and nature conservation are becoming vital, it seems strange that bull-fighting, a barbaric pursuit, should survive. Could it be that in a social psyche which believes in the existence of good and evil, good must prevail over evil – and be seen to prevail? If this idea were to be symbolically enacted in the roles played by the matador and bull: the former brave, proud, stiff-backed and calm in the face of "adversity"; the latter evil incarnate, the red burning eyes, the raw killer mien – the very epitome of the diabolical in the horns and cloven hoof, and the association of black with evil. If man and beast do in fact act these roles with such psychological overtones it could explain the continued popularity of the ritual and the spectators' gratification expressed by the near ecstatic jubilation at the climax of the event when the "evil" bull receives the coup de grace. The subjugation of evil is completed by the final humiliation of the bull's carcass being dragged around and out of the arena by his tail. From a different perspective, the bull's persecution and sublime slaughter could be interpreted as good over evil, as the sacrifice of an innocent is not unknown in human history.

To reach the museum we were obliged to cross above the bull-pens on an elevated walkway. There were several occupants in the pens (condemned cells) but one in particular noticed our passage. As Mark and I stood gazing down at them, this bull attentively returned our gaze. After about a minute we began to feel uncomfortable, and we quickly followed the ladies into the museum before we should start interpreting that look.

The bull-fighting museum portrayed a collection of the costumes worn by some of the more famous bull-fighters of the century. The tightly fitting "bolero" jackets and calf-length trousers were encrusted with intricate embroidery, and in one case, gold thread. The matador was required to be immaculately turned out on the day that could be his last. Other memorabilia such as old posters, programs and photographs adorned the walls. Also adorning the walls from which they mutely resented the curious gaze of visitors, were the mounted heads of bulls that had earned their place in the museum by their spirited performance in the ring. Adding to the sense of the macabre, one or both ears and sometimes the tail as well, were awarded the matador as a trophy.

We left the stadium with a silent echo of thousands of "ole's" in our ears and felt it was time for something in lighter vein so we set off for Senor Antonio Gaudi's artistic creations. A Spanish architect practicing around the turn of the 20th century, Gaudi (1852-1926) bequeathed to society a variety of structures: houses, tenements, garden elements, in an architectural style as unconventional in those days as it has been ever since. Showing a disdain for geometrical discipline, his works bear the marks of fairy-tale traditions: spires and turrets; tall chimneys and wavy eaves; fenestration reveals looking for all the world like entrances to caves; textures of finishes coarse and unexpected; the straight line abhorred; glazed ceramic decoration to roofs, walls and window sills, all of which create a "gingerbread-house" effect. It was perfectly clear why Gaudi had been commissioned to design a children's park (Guell Park) because of his obvious flair for producing work of an intensely human and personal nature. His piece de resistance however must be "La Sagrada Familia" (The Temple of the Holy Family). This monumental work of staggering proportion (the nave is 45m wide), was commenced in 1882 and is yet incomplete. Work has proceeded fitfully, perhaps due to the financial and technical demands of such a gargantuan project. Currently the façade, known as the "Birth Front" for its portrayal of the nativity, stands as a city landmark with its four 100 metre high perforated towers. Crowned with large ceramic stars, the towers appear like huge sculpted candles. Attached to walls are strange and fascinating creatures: climbing, crawling, creeping; snails, snakes, toads and tortoises; its originality is challenged only by its symbolic obscurity. We visited the museum on the site and gazed in awe at a scale model of the completed church. A huge tower is planned to rise above the altar and when surmounted by a cross will dwarf the present towers. One feels that another century (or two?) will pass before the church stands complete. Also on display in the museum are the actual models created by Gaudi in the development of details: finials, capitals and arches. Although an entrance fee was charged "toward building costs", it was only as we were leaving that we noticed the sign: "Please guard the ticket to show it to the placeman at the exit". Somehow this harmonized with the Gaudi Influence which has the effect of up-ending one's ideas of the conventional.

En route to the Ramblas, we were entertained in an underground Metro station by a group of busking musicians, very talented in producing "hot" Spanish sounds. The Ramblas is a broad boulevard reserved for pedestrians and here folk of all descriptions stroll about to see and be seen amid numerous stalls vending flowers, trinkets, birds and books. At the lower end, on the waterfront, a bronze Christopher Columbus stares disbelievingly westward towards that elusive India from atop a tall, hollow, steel tower. One is able to gain the same view as Chris by ascending the shaft in a miniscule lift. The tower is flexible enough to sway perceptibly in a breeze and this usually discourages tourists from overstaying their visit at the viewing platform. Permanently berthed nearby is a full-scale replica of Columbus's flagship: the caravel "Santa Maria", not much bigger than a medium sized yacht.

It was now after 9:30 pm, darkening, and time to wend our weary way back to the camper. Four factors caused us to take an hour and a half to reach the spot where we had parked. i) a fairly long journey in the underground ii) inadvertently travelling two stops past our "station" iii) from the "wrong" station walking a further 500 metres in the wrong direction through dark and deserted streets in an industrial area iv) having been correctly directed, finding ourselves literally "on the wrong side of the tracks" – the camper lay on the other side of a railway line which could not be crossed due to a three metre high continuous security fence. After we had walked a goodly distance to the nearest station where we could cross the line, accompanied by malcontented mutterings regarding my lack of navigational skill, we eventually reached familiar surroundings. Our leading thought was to pile wearily into the camper, drive back to the campsite and hence to bed. However, the patron saint of travelers decreed otherwise. The day was to finish with a bang and the bang would be the smashing of a side window of the camper – but we did not know this yet.

As we approached the vehicle we noticed that a police car had parked alongside with blue light flashing. Apprehension and alarm hurried us to the scene. I thought (illogically) since it was almost 11 pm) that the police were about to tow away the camper due to a parking violation. After announcing ourselves as the owners of the vehicle to the two police officers present, we surveyed the situation. The sliding door of the camper was open revealing an interior that had been ransacked. Clothes and kitchen implements lay strewn about; sleeping bags were jumbled together with pillows; the contents of sponge-bags had been tipped out onto the floor, and the sight of her toothbrush thrown down so disrespectfully and un-hygienically triggered a savage reaction in Peggy's breast. She turned on the culprit, who had been bundled into the police car, with a ferocity that must have made him thankful that he was safely in police custody.

The scene and its aftermath was surrealism of high order. The camper with its broken window and contents in disarray; our attempt to communicate with the police in every language known to us except Spanish; the police speaking only Spanish; a dejected felon slumped resignedly in custody; everyone's complexion intermittently taking on a blue cast like the venous throbbing of faces in a weird Salvador Dali tableau, as the police light psychedelically swept the "stage" in lighthouse fashion. Eventually one of the policemen and Melody met on common ground with broken French. It transpired that the villain, a Moroccan, had forced an entry, packed various valuables mainly belonging to Mark (rather ironically as he was the most impecunious of the party), into an airline bag and had then.........FALLEN ASLEEP on the back seat of the camper. The police patrol first noticed him at about 5 pm and when they returned after 10:30 to find him still asleep, they investigated further and discovered the broken window. The police had just arrested the potential thief when we came galloping up. We were requested to follow their car to the police station so that a charge could be laid. The scene at the station was in keeping with events thus far as we tried to understand and be understood, while all manner of human flotsam stood, sat or lay in the reception lobby. Our man was duly booked and we were requested to return the following morning to make a formal statement. Anticipating further Babylonian-language confusion (correctly as it turned out) I conveyed the idea to the policemen that we should perhaps just drop the whole thing, as we were leaving Barcelona in the morning. The policeman pointed out that without a statement, a charge could not be laid and the police work resulting in the arrest would have been in vain. This had hardly been a major "bust" but eventually I agreed. To ensure our return in the morning, the police decided to keep the "loot" that had almost been stolen as evidence, but would be returned after the statement had been given. We drove back to the campsite well after midnight and the patron saint of Eventful Days gave us a dense fog as we left the city. It was generously decreed however that we would not lose our way and before long we were enveloped in welcome sleep. It took about two anxious hours to make a police statement the following day and was only made possible by the good offices of a Spanish speaker at the South African Consulate. The three-way telephone conversation that followed had the desired result (what a relief to hear English spoken), we were reunited with our "evidence" and could now leave.

There was one last visit to make before leaving Barcelona – to view an exhibition of the work of the surrealist artist Salvador Dali. His work had been chronologically arranged along a wall of the gallery so as to portray his artistic development from age 10. We found Dali's art to be provocative, mystical, bizarre, bewildering, sometimes obscene – and extremely talented. Although difficult to analyze one's response to such unconventional art, it is certainly not a simple dichotomous "like" or "dislike". As with all good art, emotional indifference is absent and complacency and conditioning are undermined.

The next destination was inland, to the small principality of Andorra, sandwiched high in the Pyrenees between Spain and France, and governed jointly by them. Our overnight stop at Ripoll was spent in a river-side campsite with a finely mown lawn along the bank. It soon became apparent why the lawn was so trim. The proprietor was employing the natural talents of a small flock of sheep moved across the grounds by means of a mobile pen. Next day we crossed into Andorra and at the border town it became obvious that Andorra was an extremely popular place. Swarms of visitors, mainly French, crowded the streets; and this was typical of the towns on the main route through the little principality. It appeared that the main attraction was more in the commercial benefits of duty-free shopping than in the charm of the countryside. Businesses proclaimed their wide range of merchandise by means of huge banners and posters which fluttered in the breeze much like national flag-day in the State of Consumerism. Radios, TV sets, watches, cameras and all the electronic paraphernalia that seems to gush unendingly out of the Far East plus: liquor by the litre; cigarettes by the carton; trivia by the ton. All the towns we passed through were like so many vast supermarkets. Between towns the scenery was ruggedly grand with occasional patches of snow lying in the clefts at higher altitudes. Hillsides were wooded and the rivers hinted at another side to Andorra, off the beaten track. We located a campsite one block off the main road in the centre of Les Escaldes, a town that seemed to be an extension of the principal town Andorra la Vella. This conjunction results in a long shop-lined main street where we amused ourselves by window-shopping (fruit liqueurs, brandies, R1 per bottle). Later that evening we followed a street parade comprising baton-whirling, high-throwing, cart-wheeling young girls dressed in leotards, a contingent of drum-majorettes and the rear brought up by a brass band that had a particularly enthusiastic drum section. The tune "Viva Espana" was played repeatedly and I wondered whether this was due to a limited repertoire, or was this a musical political statement? Whichever, it was a pleasant diversion. Imagine, as we were leaving Andorra we came face to face with President Paul Kruger. Yes the venerable Oom Paul. Well perhaps not quite so much face to face as face to billboard. There in a two metre high head and shoulders portrait was Oom Paul replete with shiny top hat and morning coat, calmly enjoying his curved pipe. He was surrounded by the words: "Paul Kruger. J.C.Kegg & Co. Zaandam-Holland". The intention of the billboard was to stimulate sales of a product described as "El Millor Formatge de Hollands" and pictured below was a large, round, red wheel of cheese.

We decided to head for the Atlantic coast via the hinterland of Spain, and then eastwards back into France. There was simply not the time to see more of Spain, not to mention Portugal; perhaps next time. The road down the mountain back into Spain passed into the plain (where contrary to popular rumour, it did not in fact rain). The colourings of the countryside were shades of sepia and russet – Shakespeare described it well: "tawny Spain". Red-tiled, white-washed villages simmered in the heat. We would not have been surprised to encounter Don Quixote and Sancho Panza by the roadside. As it happened, we encountered a large crowd of people clustered on a bridge and along the banks of one of the few rivers in this semi-arid region. Along with the others we gazed expectantly upstream, but unlike the others, we had no idea what we were waiting for. After a while we located an English speaking Spaniard (he'd worked in South Africa previously) who explained that an event was being re-enacted on the river, to commemorate the "old" method of floating timber logs from the afforested highlands, tied together as rafts, and bound for the sea 300 kilometres away. It was last done in 1931. After 15 minutes under a sweltering sun, there appeared in the distance two rafts of logs, each steered by two men using an out-rigged log as rudder. As the mini-flotilla neared the bridge, the crown broke into spontaneous applause which the men graciously acknowledged as they were swept beneath the bridge. We could discern that they were elderly gents and it was likely that this had been their trade in their youth.

It was a long, hot drive for much of the day and after passing Lerida we decided to make for Huesca in the province of Aragon, which on the map looked well off the beaten track. A few kilometres before reaching Huesca we noticed a ruined castle brooding on a knoll not far off the road. An exploration was definitely called for so we resolved to return the following morning before leaving. At the well-appointed campsite in town we voted for a cooling dip in the camp swimming pool. We had not been in the water for long when the camp supervisor appeared at the poolside and remonstrated with us in an emotional manner. Not having the vaguest notion as to his complaint, but observing his continuous reference to the poolside shower stall, we eventually gathered that the correct procedure here is to shower <u>before</u> entering the water. It was too late for that now so we made "non comprendo" gestures and left it at that. Later at the camp restaurant we indulged in "tortillas" which turned out to be scrambled egg on rolls – less exotic than we had expected.

Next morning: back to the castle. The buildings were clearly very old and were extensively ruined although some restoration was being undertaken. The surrounding countryside was bleak and forbidding: scant vegetation, rocky outcrops and gloomy "arroyos". Surprisingly intact were detailed cornices in the banqueting hall, no doubt preserved by the vaulted roof still partially in place, albeit precariously. We had a good look round and a scratch in the earth outside the walls where we turned up many glazed and unglazed potsherds and tiles. We breakfasted in the camper overlooking the castle and speculated about a time when the lord was master, his vassals doing his bidding and the serfs living as best they could.

Huesca is situated halfway between the Mediterranean Sea and the Atlantic Ocean to the north-west and as we progressed towards the latter the vegetation became increasingly verdant. We passed through large sun-flower farms and the broad sweep of yellow, like congealed sunshine, was a delight to the eye. Here, strange granite dome rock formations (like a mini Greek Meteora); and there a deserted hilltop village slowly decaying – the result of famine?... disease?...or, more likely, the lure of the "bright lights" of a big city where hoped-for financial opportunities abound and rural poverty is left behind.

In the province of Navarre we stopped briefly in the town of Pamplona. We were a few months too early for the event for which the place is principally known – the running of the bulls through the streets to the bull-ring; so instead we enjoyed a light lunch at an almost deserted square. As with other warmer Mediterranean countries, activity grinds to a halt during the midday hours of "siesta". The journey from here showed a distinct change of vegetation. Harsh dryness became lush undergrowth and this indicated the change to a coastal climate and a very different rainfall pattern, which would be confirmed later that evening.

San Sebastian is an attractive port on the Bay of Biscay, with its own crescent bay in the centre of which lies a wooded islet. A sea swelling rhythmically into frothing breakers assured us that this was not the Mediterranean. There was even a surfer working the foam and this excited Mark not a little (his own surfboard had been mothballed back in Durban). The first campsite we tried was full but we found a place in the second, and had no sooner arrived when a tremendous thunderstorm broke over the city. Lightning crackled across a grey sky ahead of rolling thunder like a conductor's electrical baton leading in the tympani. Quite a few back-packers sought shelter in the ablution blocks that night after their tents had failed the "weather test". On exploring the old harbor the following morning, we did at last come across Don Quixote and Sancho Panza – one metre tall, in bronze, on a pedestal, decorating a circular flower garden. Again we felt the charm exerted by the old haunts of seamen: cobbled streets, tiny houses, a tiny haven just big enough to admit a fishing smack. The fishing accoutrements were there - nets, floats, anchors, coils of rope – but these symbols were clearly passing from a position of economic necessity towards obsolescence, or at best, tourist attractions. Twentieth century technology has provided civilized man with an easy living and sea-front vendors supplying sea-food victuals are now a tourist curiosity.

BACK TO FRANCE

With 21 weeks under the belt and 5 to go, we crossed the frontier back into France. At Jean de Luz we had lunch on a cliff-top overlooking a wild and turbulent sea. Vast slabs of rock dipped near vertically, as if the sea had undermined the edge of the continent causing it to collapse. A short way further we found a beautiful campsite at Biarritz. The large grounds were wooded with many ornamental trees, but most striking were the huge banks of blue, pink and white hydrangeas which separated the pitches. The cause of this verdancy manifested itself shortly after our arrival – another torrential thunderstorm. Before settling in for the evening we replenished groceries at the "Geant" (Giant) supermarket nearby. We were again struck by the modernity of the super-stores found in France; located in even the most unlikely rural area. Stocking just about everything for a comfortable epicurean lifestyle the customer has choices way beyond what we had been accustomed to. Next morning we strolled through Biarritz, a sea-side resort which rose to snobbish respectability in the 19th century by the patronage of Empress Eugenie, wife of Napoleon III. Her summer palace is today a hotel, painted in elegant shades of cinnamon.

We moved northwards on a secondary road through many kilometres of cool, coastal pine forest: the floor carpeted with luxuriant ferns. This region, Les Landes (the moors or plains) is afforested to the extent of eight hundred thousand acres. In the marsh areas the shepherds are obliged to "walk" on wooden stilts, but we did not witness this. Vineyards and villages; farmyards and fields; as we passed along we glimpsed a life of pastoral serenity, long forgotten in the cities. We skirted sprawling Bordeaux and at Royan found a lovely campsite. As well as thick lawn-grass underfoot, here were orchards of apple and pear trees and an interesting oak wood. Gypsy-like, we were soon foraging for fresh fruit (our philosophy that fruit trees within a campground were fair game had not changed) and we laid in several days' stock. Peggy stewed the apples because they were hard, and revealing an improvisation developed by our gypsy life-style, served up the stewed apples garnished with the traditional herb of cloves – toothache drops "borrowed" from the first-aid box.

We moved out early next morning and stopped for breakfast at the fortified harbor of La Rochelle. Another very old port, two 14th century towers flank the harbor mouth between which could be stretched heavy iron chains should there be a threat to the town from the sea. Along the seafront, behind a defensive wall, ancient houses press together as if for safety. Along a quay a bustling market attracted passersby and tried to sell them sea-food snacks, jewelry or leather goods. A few kilometers distant lay the modern harbor and we caught a glimpse of the huge, sinister looking concrete structures built by the Germans four decades ago to house and maintain their U-boats.

At St. Nazaire the Loire flows broadly into the sea over which we soared on an impressive cable-stayed bridge. We felt as if we were riding the back of a rainbow as we rose high above the water on the steeply arched deck. The promontory beyond St. Nazaire has been romantically named Cote d'Amour and at the seaside town of La Baule we stopped to inspect a magnificent carousel. Dressed in glistening primary colours, the horses patiently awaited their young riders in disciplined rows. Then off they would go! As the circular platform gained momentum, so did they swing into that characteristic motion as they bobbed up and down their poles in the manner universally adored by youngsters (and oldsters). Gaily painted scenes of strange, yet somehow familiar, landscapes passed by as we watched. Traditional fairground music accompanied the procession of mock carriages surrounded by ranks of cavalry. The very name "carousel", which means "military pageant", seemed to suggest that we were witnessing in the merry-go-round a fossilized representation of the past when equestrian military was paramount. Were those the fifes and drums subtly tucked away in the music?

A few kilometres further we encountered a medieval town "Guerand", in "good working order", its defensive perimeter wall intact. Gay bunting dressed the shops where local wines and farm produce were on sale. We found a small campsite with neatly trimmed lawns at Herbignac which proved to be the cheapest on our trip – R 4,20 for the five of us. Nearby lay the bones of a ruined chateau. The skeletal outline of crumbling towers and walls were softened by the lush encroachment of creepers and undergrowth, and velvety, green sheen of algae on the stagnant moat.

Now in Brittany, we followed the coastline for the short hop to what must be one of the most intriguing pre-historic sites in Europe: the "menhir" alignments at Carnac. As we were to learn, a menhir (long stone) is a roughly hewn slab of solid rock. Thousands were quarried, dressed, transported and embedded into the earth: in rows; in circles; in isolation; to stand as …..what? Anthropologists guess at meanings sepulchral, military, religious, astronomical, even phallic, yet all seems to be conjecture – a puzzle that may never be solved. Indeed what could the purpose of our Neolithic ancestors, of six millennia distant, have been when they deemed it desirable to implant the rows of upright stones, now known as the Alignments? At Carnac, over a thousand inscrutable menhirs stand regularly spaced, varying in height from eighty centimeters to a towering six and a half metres (weighing hundreds of tons) and forming weird parallel megalithic avenues more than a kilometre in length. As well as these sentinels of a past age, we also inspected the "dolmens" – tunnels and tombs formed by large slabs of flat rock placed across the tops of opposing rows of menhirs. Interestingly, archeologists have discovered stone-age remains across the length and breadth of Europe and elsewhere in the world. It is a fact that most of the pottery ever made by man, since containers were invented, is still in existence – either whole or as potsherds, due to the durability of baked clay.

Sorely tempted to follow the rugged Brittany coastline with its promise of exploration of bays, inlets and Breton fishing villages, Tyrant Time decided for us, so instead we headed for La Manche (English Channel) where the supposed high point of secular French architecture lay in the form of Mont St. Michel. En route we visited the port of St. Malo, an old corsair town founded on an island in the bay for defensive purposes. Its massive ramparts and fortifications were designed to provide military security against raids by the English. We spent an interesting hour in the maritime museum that displayed the memorabilia from days of yore: pirates' sea-chests; ships' wooden figureheads; models of caravelles; weaponry, anchors; uniforms and insignia; and one well documented display of a naval engagement that resulted in the capture of an English man o' war – along with her captain!

Beyond the ramparts of the town we noticed a sign that referred to one of the close in-shore islands known as Grand Be'. It informed us as follows:

WARNING

For your safety it is forbidden to go to the Grand Be' at flood tide for on the very moment, sea is within 10m of the submersible way. If you are caught by flood tide, do not come back on the shore. Stay then on the islet till the causeway is uncovered. Wait 6 hours!

What might have served us better however would have been a warning to take careful note of where you park your vehicle. It took us a half-hour to find the camper in the tight maze of crooked streets and squares that began to look quite familiar the longer we searched. If there had been snow on the ground we would have stumbled on our tracks more than once. Losing the camper was all the more odd since the extent of the fortified town was relatively confined. Suspecting an act of piracy, we at last found our home where we had left it – outside a police station flying the "tricolor". We left Dinard where we had camped in close company with scores of modern-day "gypsies", and broke our fast on a wild, almost eerie promontory, the Pointe du Grouin, where the ground was thick with bracken. A strong current surged nearby between the mainland and a grim looking island a few hundred metres off-shore.

It was a short drive to Mont St. Michel on the Normandy coast and due to well publicized photographs of this unique island we approached with excited anticipation. The sight of Mont St. Michel is truly remarkable. Although now connected to the mainland via a causeway, the "island" character is not diminished. The original abbey, founded in 708 and added to over the centuries by Normans and Goths, towers massively over the little village fringing its base. A gilded figure of the Archangel Michael is celestially poised on a soaring pinnacle. En mass the appearance is pyramid shaped and the intricately tooled sides result in many facets, planes, angles and shadows. At night the effect is startling due to the skillful lighting of the abbey. Because of the flatness of the surrounding sea-bed and large tidal range, at low tide the sea is nowhere to be seen. This condition may persist for a fortnight at certain times of the year revealing an immense "sea-bed-scape" stretching to the horizon. It is safe to walk on the sands, at low tide, and as a vestige of the once-held myth that quick-sands exist, a "quick" condition is easily generated by treading "on the spot". The water-table soon rises to the spongy surface and the treader finds himself sinking into the saturated sand. This sensation promptly terminates the experiment! It was to experience the magic of the sea making its irresistible pilgrimage to the island that decided us to await the incoming tide, high-water occurring at five minutes past midnight. We duly stationed ourselves on a battlement after sunset and commenced our vigil. Throughout the long twilight and darkening shadows there was no sign of an incoming tide. The sands continued to glint damply as the hours crawled by. Although the dark night had prevented close observation, the silence prevailing suggested nothing was happening. We made our way to the beach and to our great surprise we found an immobile sheet of water. High tide had materialized completely soundlessly. Satisfied at last, we wended wearily to the open ground where, in the company of several other campervans, we were spending the night - a night that was to engrave itself into our memories.

A few hours later we were awoken by a furious wind-storm, accompanied by torrents of rain that fiercely lashed the campervans and tents. The stygian blackness was intermittently fractured by bolts of lightning, crazing the sky and momentarily revealing the eerie presence of the unlit abbey before us. Our two pup-tents, bearing the brunt of the storm, were flapping like stranded manta rays so I moved the camper to windward to shield them, and of course, their occupants. At the first attempt the vehicle stalled and I attributed this to my three a.m. bleariness. On a second attempt I raced the engine and slipped the clutch and the camper jolted over an obstacle which I believed, no, hoped, was a stone. The night and the storm eventually moved on and daylight drew tired, but relieved, faces from the tents for a welcome cup of coffee. I then discovered that our three nested aluminium cooking pots had been the obstacle, now seriously mis-shapen. I managed however to restore them to their utilitarian, if not aesthetic, function by corrective panel-beating.

Exploring the island was thrilling, and the guided tour of the abbey (English group) was well presented and informative. Our guide was a well spoken and slightly arrogant French lady who, unbelievably, joked about the Norman Conquest to a handful of tittering English folk who clearly were not sure whether they should feel embarrassed at their "defeat", or be magnanimously forgiving of that un-neighbourly channel crossing of 1066. (If I had thought of it at the time I would have made a nonchalant reference to Henry V at Agincourt).

The present abbey, constructed in the 13th century, was quite an engineering feat in itself. The foundations were cut into solid bedrock and are visible in the crypts and cellars. The heavily buttressed walls conceal huge halls where the monks stored, prepared and consumed their meals; slept, studied and worshipped. The floors are stone flags, ceilings stone vaults or great baulks of timber, and some rooms enjoy huge fire-places. More recently, the de-consecrated abbey was used as a prison by Napoleon I for about sixty years when about twelve thousand prisoners were incarcerated.

We had vaulted across the mouth of the Loire River at St. Nazaire's arched bridge two days previously and now the Loire Valley beckoned. It meant heading south again to enter the Valley at Angers, 140 kilometres from the coast. It was a pleasant drive to Angers, passing through soft meadows and occasionally along avenues of trees thoughtfully planted by Napoleon for the shade and comfort of travelers. What the Rhine and its castles are to Germany, the Loire and its chateaux are to France. The Loire is the only major river wholly within French borders, and kings and aristocracy of past centuries selected its banks and tributaries above any other region where their fortresses, castles and palaces were to be sited. Over one hundred and twenty, in various states of disrepair, await the attentions of lovers of history, architecture, archeology, or simply something old which is something new.

At Angers we found a fortress erected by the energetic chateau builders, the family Foulques Nerra. In the 13th century, seventeen huge towers measuring eighteen metres in diameter at the base were studded into a massive defensive wall a kilometre in length. The forbidding aspect of the defences were softened by the attractive ornamental gardens which have been planted in the now dry moat; the reindeer browsing in an enclosure are an added attraction. Our route followed the river upstream along a road built atop what appeared to be flood-control dykes. As we drove, leisurely, we marveled at the unspoiled scenery: the verdant foliage on the banks; the woods; the river itself, curling lazily around sandbars and gliding softly by sandy beaches. We had the impression that we had taken a wrong turn and were driving alongside the lazy Limpopo – look there! a croc on that sandbank – no, just a log.

Pressing ever onwards along the "Chateau Route" we arrived at Saumer Chateau. Within an hour of checking into the municipal campsite, Peggy's and my own wallets had been stolen. We had no idea of how this could have happened, except our ultra-casual gypsy lifestyle had probably induced an un-alert dreaminess. She reported having had about R 64 whereas I had R 16. (How did she have four times as much as I did? Another insoluble mystery). We duly reported our loss to the police and made statements. After this low-key drama, we toured the chateau and museum. At night the chateau was tastefully illuminated, with reflections bouncing off the river.

Continuing along the Loire, with short diversions up the tributaries, we found villages where the changes associated with the passage of time were conspicuously absent. Apart from the principal asphalt roads and the sight of motorized traffic, nothing in the appearance of houses, shops, churches and, of course, the chateaux, suggested anything born of this century. We paused to admire the exteriors of many chateaux but there was neither the time nor the funds to visit the interiors of any but a few: 15th century Montsoreau, massive and formidable, built right on the river's edge; Usse', a "double" chateau: one wing a staid, monumental edifice with dormer-windows and occasional towers, the other a welter of towers and turrets, steeples and spires, chimneys and chanticleers. Tradition has it that the Chateau d'Usse' was the model used by Perrault for his fantasy story "The Sleeping Beauty".

Chinon is a town that appears to have been deliberately retained in "medieval mode", perhaps partly because of an event that took place here on 25th February 1429. On that day, the divinely inspired Jehanne Darc arrived to inform a listless and demoralized Dauphin (England had by then achieved almost total control over France) that the siege at Orleans could be raised; he, the Dauphin, would be crowned king of all France at Rheims; and that the English would be driven off French soil. As every schoolchild knows, these predictions materialized but Joan of Arc was martyred at the stake, a prisoner in the hands of the English. Somehow there was just the tiniest connection with those turbulent days as we strolled up the Rue Jeanne d'Arc to visit the chateau.

We crossed to the right bank of the Loire to see Langeais where the chateau stands unaltered since its erection by Louis XI in 1645. The original "keep" (the final sanctuary if overrun by the enemy) of the fortress built by one of the counts Foulques Nerra in the 10th century still remains, one of the oldest in France. We gazed at the stern façade: moat, drawbridge, and portcullis entrance flanked by huge and forbidding towers.

Moving on, the terrain rose into an escarpment and we found ourselves following the base of a limestone cliff up to 30 metres high in places and stretching for many kilometers. What really made us stare were the numerous dwellings that have been cut into the soft cream-coloured rockface. We were not able to date the caves but whoever those early troglodytes were, they set a trend that still flourishes today as many of the caves are in fact occupied. The rock is soft enough to work easily and rectangular rooms with inter-leading doorways have been excavated. A lack of natural light to inner rooms required the use of fuel-burning lamps as the soot blackened patches on the walls showed (what about ventilation?). Window openings had been cut into the external wall, from which chimney flues protruded, several metres higher. The overall impression one has from the outside: the curtained windows, a wooden front door, a chimney flue with a conical hood slightly awry, was one of having blundered into an alien environment. Were the inhabitants Hobbits? Dwarves? Earth folk? At one of the caves, converted to a shop, we purchased two kilograms of mushrooms that had been cultivated in the inner reaches of the establishment, and for days we enjoyed the delicious fungus with our meals. In a nearby village a placard in a real estate shop's window advertised, with a colour picture, one of the caves "to let - with all mod. cons."

The next chateau on our upstream route was at Villandry, where we camped on a site wooded, grassed and cheap. The 16th century chateau has a large square keep incorporated into one of the corners, a relic of a much older fortress. The building is U-shaped with arched colonnades facing a central court. The roof is conspicuous for its many sculpted gable and dormer windows. Even the most insensitive non-gardener would not fail to be impressed by the immaculate workmanship revealed in the extensive grounds. Three distinct types of garden have been created. The water garden centres on an ornamental lake that serves the chateau's moat and provides irrigation for the other sections. A second garden, more formal, is characterized by the distinctive geometrical patterns drawn by low hedges, immaculately clipped to form heart-shapes, crescents and scalloped enclosures and planted with a variety of flowers. Separating the hedges are neatly raked gravel paths. Topiary conifers stand in elegant pairs at intervals. The remaining garden provides the chateau kitchen (and perhaps neighbouring kitchens) with fresh vegetables and herbs. The garden is sub-divided into square and rectangular plots that have been planted with various leafy vegetables that provide patterned contrasts in colour, height and texture.

Skirting the large town of Tours, probably to our loss, we stopped at the riverside chateau of Amboise, a regal looking establishment. This is to be expected from a castle that was, in fact, the home of kings for many years. We toured part of the interior and marveled at the opulent living conditions certain members of the human tribe had managed to arrange for themselves: rich hardwoods carved into four-poster beds, chests, wardrobes, furniture, floors and ceilings. Walls painted or papered in lavish designs and often decorated with the mystical symbol, the "fleur-de-lis". This "flower-of-the-iris" adopted by French royalty as their symbol has also been found in ancient Egyptian and oriental art. The three- petalled ideogram also had associations with the concept of the Christian Trinity. Other than conventional paintings, an art form that has preserved for posterity the customs, dress and events of the middle-ages is Tapestry. Huge wall hangings show royal, military or pastoral scenes, exquisitely recorded in thread and fine textures. Sadly, an irreversible phenomenon associated with exposure to light and passage of time is reducing many medieval tapestries to a blue/green hue. Within the grounds of Amboise there lies buried the great innovator and artist, Leonardo da Vinci. His last years were spent in an outbuilding near the chateau, "le Clos-Luce'", a mansion granted him by the king.

Onward to Blois, where we would leave the Loire river. The chateau here is another fine example of artistry in architecture and decoration, and like all palaces and castles accommodating the "noble" class of humanity, is larger than life in its scale. Huge doorways and windows, high ceilings, and in general the Brobdingnagian ornamentation are intended to inspire in their subjects a suitable veneration for the stature of their ruler. It was not convenient to visit the interior of Blois, but we nevertheless enjoyed exploring the façades and in particular, an equestrian statue of Louis XII in a delightfully sculpted niche above a doorway.

We left the Loire flowing lazily in the sunshine, perhaps dreaming of days gone by when coaches and kings and cavalry rode along her banks; the magnificent chateaux drifting by with pennants snapping in the breeze, smoke pluming out of tall chimneys, knights in the halls; peasants tilling the fields; here a lady and her entourage perambulating in the gardens; there the brazen call of a hunting horn on the sighting of boar or stag.

Chartres was now our destination, a hundred kilometers to the north, to visit the 10th century cathedral built at the height of Crusading fervour. The cathedral dominates the skyline while the village huddles around its skirts in seemingly frail dependency. The front façade is remarkable for the different architectural styles of the twin towers. The right-hand tower was constructed in undecorated, almost austere verticality; while the other, built several centuries later, reveals an advanced stage of artistic and engineering development, having been confidently decorated and embellished. The towers, metres apart in space and centuries apart in time, bear mute testimony to the skill of the master-builders of the day. The great rose-windows are striking: not unlike giant kaleidoscopes held up to the sky showing patterns of colourful religiosa. Stone carvings in the choir depicting the life of Christ have been executed with breathtaking finesse. There is an esoteric pattern in the floor at the entrance of similar excellence.

Paris was drawing us toward her with magnetic subtlety, but there was one call we had to make before yielding to her promised charms. Fontainebleau. In royal days of yore, a palace was built here in magnificent forest surroundings. It is remarkable that vast forest tracts still exist in close proximity to the vast urban sprawl that is Paris. They have thankfully been spared the woodman's axe which in other parts of Europe, and particularly England, rang out continuously at the time when the insatiable maws of the engines of the industrial revolution raged for fuel. Fontainebleau is a small town, the jewel of which is the chateau, situated amid trim lawns and huge ponds. However, the forest was the primary attraction for us, and we agreed the best way to experience it would be on bicycles. These were painlessly hired at the railway station and we were soon wobbling our way into the woods complete with rucksack and picnic lunch. The afternoon was spent blissfully meandering along sand roads and bridal paths, being entertained by song-birds and soothed by the leafy tranquility of our surroundings.

The natural charm of the French, often inhibited in the bigger cities, was made manifest in the cheerful cry "bon appétit" from a passerby as we reclined in a dappled clearing enjoying a snack. Further on we encountered two French couples who had set up table and chairs, were engaged in an "al fresco" game of cards and exuded much bonhomie as we passed by. Several hours later, but all too soon, even though by then it was seven-thirty pm, we had to return the cycles. We found a lovely campsite a few kilometres further on the bank of the river Seine. The forest undergrowth had been cleared to form niches in the bush which afforded campers privacy and gave a feeling of camping "wild". We strolled along the river bank and discovered another form of unconventional lifestyle – a private barge, anchored close inshore. The cabin windows prettily dressed in chintz and flowering pot plants showed a woman's touch.

Paris! With our romantic expectations firing on all cylinders we plunged into "Gay Paree" and were not disappointed. Apart from monuments and places of interest such as the Eiffel Tower, Arc de Triomphe, the Louvre and Tuillerie Gardens, Notre Dame Cathedral, the Champs Elysees, Hotel de Ville, and so on, all most charming or dramatic as the case may be – the more so perhaps because of their reputation and familiarity – the "real" atmosphere and feeling of Paris stems from its inhabitants. The scenes played out by ordinary folk in the streets, perhaps at a pavement café, or at a street market where if it is to your taste you may buy: a snake; an iguana; a chameleon; a goat; an antelope; a kitten or puppy. If space is a problem: a gerbil; a mouse or goldfish. If street entertainment is more to your taste, find an open space and you'll be sure to see and hear: buskers; play actors; mimes; raconteurs and at least one juggling unicyclist. It is the human touch that creates a carnival atmosphere during which life's sorrows, real or imagined, may be set aside for a while. From the quiet elegance of the Louvre, the largest palace in the world, outside which busker entertainment is, appropriately, classical music; to the frenetic activity in the square adjacent to that un-endearing edifice, the surrealistic glass and bones Pompidou Centre where a dozen or more scenarios were being enacted simultaneously. Here a drama group performing an obscure work depicted by swaying soliloquies and leaping leotards; there a young man and woman, performing in mime the horrors of Hiroshima (it was the 38th anniversary of 6th August 1945). On that fateful day fire and atomic radiation descended from the heavens on you and I (in another time and place). The man was swathed in linen as he scaled the tubular super-structure of the Arts Centre with flowing gestures, while his young lady similarly clad, but with the additional adornment of simulated flesh wounds, writhed and withered in meaningful silence on the ground. Here a group of musicians ex-temporizing with sounds that only they could appreciate; there a solitary young lady enchanting a small crowd with a mimed performance created out of the fertility of her imagination. Here an African man atop a wooden crate denouncing the decadence of European civilization, in English, with a repertoire of ready and usually obscene retorts to interjectors; there two black men in tight leathers, boots and peaked caps and dead-pan expressions, revealing their talent for automatic dancing – a mechanical, robot-like jerking stiffness – their battery powered musical accompaniment causing concern to the Frenchman nearby who was vainly endeavouring to convey to his even smaller audience the latest in French humour. He occasionally came over to request that the "automatic" music be turned down only to be met with benign non co-operation. Nearby, as a bizarre backdrop, there was a large pond that contained numerous mobile floating sculptures: a huge pair of revolving red lips; an ingenious contraption that swiveled and swayed while sibilantly spurting sinuous streams; a giant heart turning on an axle. We visited the historic Les Halles market not far from the Centre and found an ultra-modern glass and aluminium shopping complex broadcasting piped classical music, a refreshing alternative to the usual muzak.

Paris! On the left bank of the Seine, near the old university, we enjoyed a supper of "couscous" in an Algerian restaurant. Next day it was a long climb to the lofty height of the Church of the Sacre Coeur (Sacred Heart) characterized by its egg-shaped domes. Situated in the shadow of this famous church, stands an unobtrusive little chapel, the oldest in France. Round the corner stands the Montmartre, the stamping ground of impressionist artists and now commercialized by droves of "al fresco" painters, some of them talented. They make a living from the tourist stream flowing through this beautifully picturesque square.

Our routine for the next few days: by Metro underground to town from our campsite at Joinville le Pont on the outskirt of Paris. Then explore by "shank's pony" till late at night. We visited the Pigalle, a district where ladies trade in transient relationships, in the area of the night-club The Moulin Rouge (The Red Mill). In this neighbourhood are the bizarre sex shops and raunchy clubs that advertise in a particularly lurid fashion. We admired the façade of the Hotel de Ville (City Hall) a baroque architectural extravagance; gazed across the Seine at the radio antenna, symbol of Paris, Eiffel's Tower (we could not afford the ascent); perambulated in and around the awe inspiring Arc de Triomphe that has been engraved on its inner surfaces with lists of Napoleon's victorious campaigns, and at our feet a permanent resident symbolizing and glorifying the unforgotten military dead: at the head of the Tomb of the Unknown Soldier an "eternal" flame burns. We could not resist the temptation of appropriating a newly placed poppy from the grave as a souvenir.

The city gardens are called the Tuilleries Jardins, and here the pace of life slows to the point of sitting, watching, strolling ice-cream in hand, and enjoying the seamanship of young and old sailing hired model yachts on a pond. We ambled up the Champs Elysees where one needs a healthy bank account just to be able to window-shop! Amid these elegant boutiques displaying their luxurious contents we noticed an unusual form of beggar. He, amongst several, sat on the pavement with his back against a wall with his jacket draped over his head, thereby obscuring his face. Several of these beggars displayed handwritten placards that described, at some length, their justification for throwing themselves upon the benevolence of society. It occurred to me that this was an ideal opportunity for those poor folk who, wishing to remain anonymous needed to supplement their income, such as cabinet ministers, archbishops, magistrates, etc. On the other hand these fellows may have unwisely handed over their credit cards to their wives for a shopping excursion on the Champs Elysees. But seriously, it sadly proclaimed that there are those whose shame at their straitened circumstance causes them to deny their own identity. A feature in common with many European capitals is the relative absence of high-rise buildings. Here, the few that had been erected are sited well away from the centre. Thus one obtains excellent panoramic views of the city from the top floor of even a four-storey building.

Notre Dame Cathedral: This jewel of sacred architecture has been set into an island pendant, held in place by the shimmering necklace of the Seine that so gracefully encircles the throat of Our Lady; the stern twin Norman towers; the vibrant rose-windows; the powerful array of statues of kings and bishops across the full width of the front façade above three huge Gothic arched doorways; the intricate carvings to the doors; the external buttresses bracing the vaulted roof which "fly" from their springings with the grace that emerges when form and function unite; the hideous gargoyles perched on balustrades whose evil expressions seem to warn the viewer of the other side of sacred; all these impressions await the appreciative visitor. In addition to her sacred duties, Notre Dame has over the centuries been the focal point for royal ceremonies and a refuge for those politically persecuted. Romanticized by Victor Hugo, the presence of Quasimodo the hunch-backed bell-ringer can be imagined skulking in the galleries above. The Cathedral of Notre Dame is a powerful crystallization of bold construction and aesthetic energy.

Simply strolling through the city brought its own delights in novel sights, sounds and smells. We almost lost Peggy in an odd manner. Suddenly standing before us was Groucho Marx, or at least an excellent copy. He glanced our way, removed a huge cigar from his mustachioed mouth, gave a toothy grin and at the same time beckoned us with crooked index finger, to follow him.. At this, he sloped off obliquely with a small entourage in tow, Pied Piper fashion. We happened to be moving in as different direction and as we moved away I conducted the usual roll-call to ensure our continued close company. Peggy was missing! Yes….there she was in the distance, another convert at Groucho's heels.

On another occasion we joined a small group of onlookers at a pavement café'. A young couple was performing a fascinating "mechanical mime". They were dressed as waiters and wore waxy, immobile expressions: a weird effect was cleverly contrived to appear as if mechanical robots had been dressed to resemble humans, rather than humans dressed as robots acting as humans.

Their unblinking eyes had a glazed appearance, and did not move in their sockets. Their limbs moved spasmodically in regular arcs through the air at constant rates and stopped abruptly with a barely perceptible shudder as the "play" in the "hinges" was dampened. There gait was a strange "gliding" action, halting and uncertain. These players riveted one's attention and I found it difficult to believe they were flesh and blood when they "came to life" at the end of the performance. There was an odd resistance to meet their eyes afterwards – was it the subliminal fear of having witnessed "un-human" beings, or simply the embarrassment of having been taken in so completely by their "deceit"?

On the Ile de Cite', one of the two major Seine islands held to be the site of the original settlement way back in the mists of time, we visited a morbid yet fascinating memorial to the Jews who had been decimated in Nazi Germany's fit of genetic megalomania. Stark concrete walls simulate a prison yard and within a small building are two mock gas-chambers. Infamous names are engraved on the walls: Auschwitz; Dachau; Buchenwald; Belsen; Treblinka. At these centres of human shame, three quarters of European Jewry were systematically murdered; approximately half the total number of the Jewish race in the world at that time. A central display with myriad tiny lamps drives home the significance of those large numbers of ill-fated humans.

We were not far from the Louvre Museum so hither we hied via the "pont vieux" (the old bridge) which sports an amazing and amusing sequence of weird-looking faces carved in stone at the base of the parapets. The Louvre is an imposing building. Begun in the 13th century, this imperial residence grew over the centuries to become the largest palace in the world by the time it was completed six hundred years later. Calls for the royal art collections to be made available for public viewing were made in the 18th century but neither Louis XV nor Louis XVI, were amenable to this idea. Perhaps this was a small example of the Royal Attitude which culminated in the Royal Prostration at the foot of Mlle. Guillotine some years later. Anyhow it was only in 1793 after the Revolution that the galleries were opened gradually to the public. Today, this museum has a fine collection of Oriental, Egyptian and Graeco-Roman antiquities, as well as sculptures, paintings and various objets d'art. The codified Laws of Hammurabi, the Babylonian king (1750 BC) were engraved in stone. These were already ancient when Greek classical perfection produced the Venus de Milo in white marble (200 BC). With Michelangelo's sensuous sculptures of "The Captives", and so much more, the Louvre is a veritable Feast of Art. There is also the painting now protected by security glazing, and before which there is always a crowd to see one of the world's most publicized paintings: Leonardo's "Mona Lisa"; or the huge canvas painted by Eugene Delacroix entitled "Liberty Guiding the People" – a vigorous portrayal of Idealistic Liberty being promoted by a busty lady striding across the fallen in battle, and proudly bearing aloft the Tricolor, setting Hope and Purpose into the lives of the People following behind. In the endless corridors one occasionally comes across an artist, fully equipped with canvas and easel, copying an Old Master. If learning is done by imitation, what finer tutors could be sought but the best?

Our Parisian sojourn was now at an end and we set our sights on Calais where we would ferry across to England. However not far from Paris lay Versailles, a "visit to which ought not to be missed" as the advertising brochure informed us. The sprawling palace built by Louis XIV in the 17th century has been described as a "monument to man's obsession with himself". We were discouraged from visiting the interior by the sight of queues of tourists snaking across court-yards towards various entrances, so instead explored the gardens. The grounds are vast to the point of overwhelming; woods alternating with ornamental ponds; lawns and flower beds. There is scarcely a pond that does not have fountains in the shape of frogs and other aquatic beasties, sprites and statues. One dynamic sculpture is of Neptune being drawn out of the water in his chariot by straining horses. We discovered that it was only on special occasions that the water-works were operated due to the high cost of electricity required. (What did Louis do?). At some distance from the main buildings there lies a sizeable lake. Rowing boats were on hire for visitors to reach the "Trianons", something like a summer-house. Louis could accommodate ten thousand people at Versailles, including five hundred servants. Noblemen and women of various rank he deliberately caused to become dependent on the royal favour for their well-being. This was to prevent intrigue against the royal person. Apollo, in the aspect of Sun God was the favourite of Louis, and while he did not go so far as to call himself a Sun God, he modestly let it be known that he was the Sun King. Louis was endowed with a not inconsiderable measure of self-esteem, and it was customary for him to be attended by nobles who, for the hour, were specially favoured. Court life revolved about Louis's presence and actions. Every morning a buzz would ripple through the palace: "The king is awake!", and the especially favoured were permitted to watch the king, rise, dress and breakfast. No doubt by missing the tour of the interior, we forewent a glimpse of regal affluence without equal in Europe.

We made an overnight stop en route to the coast at a small village with a folksy name; Beautangles. We camped among trees with lush grass underfoot adjoining a chateau. This was unfortunately not open to visitors but we admired the building through the wrought-iron gates which were elaborately decorated with hunting motifs.

The following afternoon we arrived at the port of Calais. The day was blustery and overcast, but we had the time and inclination to explore the town. We admired the "story-book" red-brick town hall and its elaborately decorated clock tower. At the beachfront a young man provided Mark and I with vicarious thrills as he sent his sand-yacht skittering across the damp sand at high speed. The sea was murky, grey and choppy, with ferries scudding in and out of the harbor entrance. Outside a beer-garden nearby, I noticed a signboard advertising the following: "9 SPECIALITIES OF BEER. 5 ARE STRANGER", also "Served at all times English waiters". As vegetarians they would have to get by without our custom, and we passed by. For reasons of economy we chose the channel crossing departing at 00:15 hours, for Dover. Even at this unearthly hour the ferry charge for the hour-long trip across the English Channel was almost equal to the fare for the 24 hour crossing from Brindisi, Italy to Patras, Greece. This well indicates the cost of living difference between the geographical extremes of the European Economic Community.

TO ENGLAND

The white cliffs of Dover skulked yellowy in the glare of the port lights as the ferry approached this British Island. Ashore, we greatly enjoyed hearing the natives speak the first intelligible language since leaving South Africa, five and a half months previously – English. A similar way of life and strong cultural connections between South Africa and England produced in us a benign familiarity as our tour progressed. One of these connections is the practice of driving on the left hand side of the road, a habit I had to re-learn as matter of urgency. Outside Dover, road signs in French and English remind drivers at regular intervals to keep left.

After sleeping away the few remaining hours of the night of our arrival in a lay-bye off the road in company with assorted heavy trucks, we drove on to Canterbury, a delightful medieval village. The Norman-towered cathedral, for centuries the focus of pilgrimages, contains several royal tombs as well as "the very spot", suitably marked on the floor, where the archbishop Thomas a' Beckett was assassinated in 1170; that is today stared at by visitors with macabre relish, no doubt imagining bloodstains. The main street leading off from the cathedral precincts was strung with pennants adding a festive touch to the Tudor houses and quaint shops, the front doors of which tinkle a welcome to all who enter. We pressed on for London through rolling green countryside and by the afternoon had found a good campsite at Crystal Palace, fifteen kilometres from the City. The campground is located on the site of the huge Victorian glass-clad exhibition hall which was razed by fire in the twenties. Joanna left us at this stage to visit relatives of hers in London prior to returning to South Africa independently. "Goodbye Joanna, we enjoyed your company for the past 5½ months". From our campsite, as was our custom in large towns and cities, we made use of public transport to avoid the traffic found in "town driving" and putting the campervan and its contents at risk (remember Barcelona!). From Crystal Palace our bus fare to town at 75p each meant that we were paying about R 11 for the four of us to which had to be added occasional tube fares making London travel costly.

London, steeped in tradition and history, is a city that has spread over the centuries, devouring villages and boroughs to wax fatly as "Greater London", 800 square kilometres in area. There is something for everyone in London and it is difficult to imagine a human interest or activity that is not catered for by way of club, institution or group of "afficionados" without even mentioning the representation of man's and the earth's history, artifacts and achievements, to be explored at the plethora of museums and galleries.

The sprawling parks provide recreational escape from the bustle of a throbbing metropolis: the mellow tranquility of St.James's Park with its reedy notes floating across from the military bandstand; to the "piece of countryside" that is Regent's Park where the London Zoo is situated; or huge Hyde Park: sailing on the Serpentine, riding in Rotten Row or being entertained by the pontificating at Speaker's Corner. Here the principle of "free speech" provides an opportunity for frustrated would-be politicians and lay orators to regale their audiences from "soap-boxes" and step-ladders with such topics as: left-wing politics; right-wing politics; religion; racism; atheism; socialism; nationalism; patriotism and a bag-full of other "isms". The audience gets its own back with a high and often amusing standard of heckling and disruptive comment, which has the effect of preventing the speakers, and the audience, from taking it all too seriously. To discourage the hecklers themselves from taking it too seriously, the ubiquitous Bobby is there to ensure that speakers are not prevented from speaking by excessive interjections, and we saw several instances where police action was taken to protect Freedom of Speech as speech saboteurs were led away to cool off. No subject is taboo, within the bounds of deliberate incitement or personal slander and many speakers showed a professional polish and ready wit.

To participate as a speaker, he arrives with a portable platform or small step-ladder, erects it, climbs above the general head-level of the spectators, and begins to speak, without a trace of inhibition. What he says may be true or false or a mixture; outrageous or boring; it may be a topical subject or merely relate to his pet theories or hobby; or an outpouring of a disordered mind like the gentleman neatly attired in a suit and tie who attempted to recruit neuro-surgeons from passers-by, and then veered off to explain the principles of space flight in colourful and illogical terms. A large crowd had gathered around a man in a cloth cap who had decorated his pitch with a large red flag. His subject was communism and as he grew increasingly passionate about his subject, gobs of sputum started flying about with his vehemence. A bowler-hatted city gent stood nearby with a furled umbrella, and with great presence of mind, opened the brolly over his head to ward off the flying sputum. This raised a huge laugh, not least from the orator. Or the long-haired, bearded young man wearing a beatific expression who calmly proclaimed to his audience: "You rejected me when I visited this planet two thousand years ago, and you are rejecting me now........". (Pregnant silence ...). The audience collapsed with mirth when an elderly lady pushed her way up to him, jabbed him several times in the ribs with the tip of her umbrella and said in a stern voice: "Cut your hair and get a job!" Even the pseudo-messiah cracked a smile. Or the pimply "punk" having an intense discussion with a "straight" executive type on the subject of his, the punk's, validity as a human being and whether his living as provided by the State in the form of dole, was justifiable. The argument seemed to concern the division of responsibility between State and Individual with respect to the harmonious ordering of Society. Then there was the cleric, enthusiastically spreading "the Good News", repeatedly interrupted by a non-descript, plain little man. The interjections were not of the good-natured heckling variety, but were mocking, malicious and vitriolic. The cleric suddenly turned on his opponent with the full force of his attention and said quietly: "I know who you are. I recognize you here before me. You are the Devil!" These words had a strange effect on the man. He dropped his gaze and "slunk" away through the crowd – simply melting away. Peggy, who had been observing this interchange, noticed that he did not join the audience of any of the other speakers, but left the park altogether.

At Speaker's Corner one had only to reveal one's nationality as South African to invite interested comment and questions such as: "Why do you treat your blacks so badly?" On one occasion I was obliged to rescue Melody from an Irishman who had cornered her with this question, although by the tone of the conversation it may have been the Irishman that I was rescuing, as I dragged Melody away.

The inhabitants of London present a diverse portrait: blacks, speaking with cockney accents; whites, speaking with accents that defy classification; browns, wearing a burnous, yashmak or sari; youths wearing their hair like nightmarish cranial topiary: in tufts, tassles, stripes and spikes, dyed in pastel shades of pink and green, bleached snow-white or artistically sprayed in overlapping rainbow colours. Some bore an uncanny resemblance to a sucked out mango pip. (Anyone who has really enjoyed a succulent mango would have ended up with a pip with stiff hairy fibres radiating outwards like the rays of the sun). The "sucked mangoes", as we came to call them, offered to pose for tourist photographs at a fee of 20p or so. Their apparel harmonized perfectly: torn jeans and tee shirts, heavy boots and matching accessories: badges, symbols and tattoos. Great study material for sociologists and psychology students. Especially notable was the "sucked mango" who passed us on the pavement in full regalia, swinging a blaring portable radio, and as the ultimate fashion accessory to his "haute couture" had clinging to his shoulder a rat dyed a matching bright pink.

Of course in cities harbouring souls by the million, the occasional "odd-ball" is to be expected as Melody discovered while she was photographing St. Paul's Cathedral. While peering through the viewfinder she became aware of an elderly man passing by who launched into a tirade of invective directed towards her. Melody gaped and gasped while he continued to rail at her, gesticulating wildly as he proceeded on his way. On the same occasion, Peggy, in chatting to a British policeman on the steps of St. Paul's, asked why the British Public put up with the apparently unfair system of taxation that provided unemployment relief, dole, for "sucked mangoes" and the like who, as they readily admit, are unemployable as a result of their bizarre appearance. Did the good bobby allow her a glimpse of the British "skeleton-in–the-cupboard" with his rejoinder: "Because we're stupid!"?

There are many fine monuments, shrines and attractions to be enjoyed in London. The perfect proportions of Christopher Wren's Cathedral in honour of St. Paul – the frescoes painted within the dome deliberately distorted to compensate for the perspective of double curvature as seen from floor level; the awesome Westminster Abbey, wherein is buried many of the nation's famous, and where Britain's era of military imperialism is etched in the numerous tributes paid to war leaders who fell in the struggle for colonial conquest: the seizure of the West Indies; the subjugation of India in the creation of the British Raj; the Zulu campaigns followed by the South African War, and similar activities across the globe which resulted in atlases showing a preponderance of red (co-incidentally the colour of blood) – the extent of the Empire – as if the world were a great colouring-in book in the minds and purposes of the empire builders. Nelson's statue, with fixed stare at the Thames Estuary, stands in his "crow's nest" on top of a column fifty metres above the square that celebrates his triumph over the combined French and Spanish fleets at Trafalgar. There is the impressive Egyptian Obelisk towering above the Thames Embankment, which broke its tow-line during a storm in the Bay of Biscay while en route to England, but later recovered with difficulty. The Tower of London, a huge fortification built over Roman defenses, the foundations of which were laid during Julius Caesar's occupation, that has been used at various times as a prison and royal apartments (we could not afford the exorbitant entrance fee to tour the interior). Street buskers were noticeable by their rarity in contrast with the street entertainments of Paris, which city, as a result could be described as more of a relaxed "fun" city than London, from a tourist perspective anyway.

There is a daily fanfaronade outside Buckingham Palace as the guard is changed: stiff-backed, red-jacketed warriors marching to "Pomp and Circumstance" type music and wearing tall bear-skin head-dress (hopefully synthetic) and mirror-polish boots clacking on the paving in unison. A visit to the docks rewarded us by the sight of "The Discovery", Captain Scott's ship that afforded him a one-way voyage to the Antarctic. This tragic event was brought home to us forcibly when we read his last words recorded in his actual diary, displayed in a glass case in the British Library. At one of the old, disused dock entrances I noticed a small plaque set in the wall: "Ivory Dock" and I wondered what these docks were like in centuries past. Here surely linger the ghosts of the press-gangs; sweating stevedores; bustling chandlers; Old Salts with many a yarn to spin of adventure, exploration, slavers and pirates, hardships and scurvy; the cargoes of Indian and African ivory ("Ivory Dock" said the sign); other cargoes from strange and exotic places; the rough-and-ready lifestyle of the "wharf rats", the hectic excesses in the taverns where memories had to be packed aboard a man's mind to see him through the long, lonely months at sea; stern-faced captains who exercised the rigid discipline that was necessary to ensure the crew's obedience when rat-lines had to be scaled, yards teetered along and canvas furled in the teeth of a rising gale. Today modern commercial docks further downstream cater for the movement of cargo and the old docks with their memories slip quietly into obscurity, awaiting whatever urban- renewal destiny lies in store for them.

During our daily bus rides we enjoyed reading billboard advertising because of their often clever or unusual messages. A couple of notices outside churches caught my eye. One said: "Come inside for a faith lift", another: "Know Jesus, know peace; no Jesus, no peace". Entertaining activity, and free, is window-shopping along Regent and Oxford Streets, Burlington Arcade and the somewhat outdated "Carnabie Street", all of which the ladies enjoyed. And there was Piccadilly Circus, a traffic round-about in a busy part of town and home to a delicate bronze statuette of the Greek god of Love, Eros. He seemed somewhat depressed however, by the unromantic circumstance of being perpetually orbited by smelly metal satellites, in the shadow of towering buildings with neon images beetling unsentimentally across their brows.

Very popular on Sundays is the Portabello Road flea-market, known colloquially as Petticoat Lane, where policemen at the access points hand out leaflets warning against the presence of pick-pockets. This brought to mind my Roman bus encounter, and I smiled knowingly at the bobby as I walked away with my copy. Petticoat Lane comprises mainly pavement stalls and much of the merchandise bears the "Made in Hong Kong" or "Made in Taiwan" stamp. Vendors were demonstrating household "gimmicks" the virtues of which were to "cut glass" or "clean up stains" or meet a thousand other household challenges: the sales pitch delivered with practiced smoothness. There were also the unlicensed peddlers who made extravagant claims for their dubious products and at the approach of a bobby showed remarkable dexterity in dismantling their pitch and adopting a look of innocence until the "threat" had passed.

With the end of our "gypsy" travels now only seventeen days away, we could not stay longer than the five already spent in London without forfeiting the further pleasure of exploring other regions in the country. First, however, a brief stop at Hampton Court palace a short distance up the river Thames. This rather austere 16th century residence was built for the Cardinal Wolsey who, when the breeze of disfavor wafted toward him as a result of his attempted conspiracy with the Pope, presented the property to King Henry VIII in an attempt (unsuccessfully) to mollify him. This attempt at goodwill did not prevent the worthy Cardinal from being charged with high treason. The palace is a unique blend of Baroque, Tudor and Victorian architecture. Christopher Wren added several wings that, strangely, reveal no attempt at integration into the existing design: the later extensions simply abutting the original construction. There are many cobbled courtyards, a profusion of chimney-stacks and Tudor kitchens with huge fireplaces. We visited the world's first tennis court, called at the time "Real", or "Royal" tennis. A match was in progress and as we watched a feeling of being transported centuries back in time washed over us. The original game was played much like present day squash-rackets in that the side and back walls were used, although the players faced each other over a net in the modern way. The Hampton Court grounds are large, well tended and gaily coloured by flowers. A noteworthy feature is a grape vine that had been planted in 1768, still fruit-bearing, and trained to form an overhead canopy. The area beneath had been cordoned off to prevent thousand of tourists' tramping feet from compacting the ground to the detriment of the extensive root system. The famous Maze in the gardens was an experience of anxious a-maze-ment. Every turn in the pathways among the neatly trimmed 2½ metre high hedges was virtually identical in appearance and our sense of direction rapidly disintegrated after a few confident turns had led into a cul-de-sac. We repeatedly encountered confused expressions on the faces of fellow mazers, no doubt bearing similar expressions on our own. The net result was a general milling about by all: "this way…", "no, this way…". It was less amusing for a young boy-scout (pathfinder?) of about eight years who had lost his companions and his way: "But I'm sure they went this way" he sobbed to an adult scout-master (of a different group) who reassured him:

"Don't worry son, we'll find them", the expression on his face contradicting the confident tone of his voice.

One of the adjectives that typify the English predilection for understatement is the word "great". In the context of Windsor Great Park, "Vast" should be substituted for "Great". In a pencil-straight line from the "front door" of Windsor Castle, the road runs into the Park for several kilometres. The Queen of the Realm was "at home" as the Union Jack fluttering at the masthead advised. We spent a while in the Park watching model aeroplanes being radio-controlled by a local club outing, and then sought a place to turn in for the night. We could not find a campsite in the vicinity, so I was all for camping in the Park. This suggestion was vigorously resisted by Peggy who prophesied a "run in" with the Royal Gamekeeper. We ended up in a suburban street in Windsor for the night, Mark sharing the front seat with the steering wheel, hand brake, and other sleep-inhibiting protuberances. Next morning, after ablutions at the railway station, we enjoyed a pleasant stroll through the village of Windsor and nearby Eton. We paused briefly outside the well-known Eton Boys' College to admire the old buildings in their garb of mellow, red face-brick amid flagged walks, all under a gentle hush of the summer vacation. As a parting memory of Windsor Castle, we watched the Queen's Guard arrive for the changing ceremony with military band in the van, fifes shrilling a warning to keep clear ahead, and the metronomic thump of the bass drum ensured a unanimous heavy "crunch" each time the Guards' heels struck the tarmac.

Travelling northwest we arrived at Oxford where we stopped for lunch on a convenient river bank. Several prettily decorated houseboats rounded off a charming setting. We drove into this medieval town, home to some thirty-six colleges collectively known as Oxford University. We spent a few relaxing hours rambling among the venerable college buildings, heavy with an air of bookish learning even though deserted for the holidays. Forgotten little notices on pin-boards informed of those events that helped to make up the daily round of college life: to be torn down unceremoniously when the college begins to stir after its summer hibernation. Many colleges have been in continuous use since their foundation in the middle ages and the ghosts of (mental) Sweat and Toil seemed to hover about the dusty classrooms. Staircases silently sloped into upper regions, the hollows in their stone treads proclaiming the passage of feet innumerable over the centuries. The number and quality of bookshops in the town is a bibliophile's paradise and, while browsing in one, I casually came across several books hundreds of years old. Prices ranged from about ten pounds upwards for these collectors' gems.

We moved on through the verdant countryside which is so characteristic of England in summertime: green fields; fat cows; Shetland ponies and brick houses with flower-covered trellises, arriving later that day at the remarkable town of Shakespeare-upon-Avon, oops sorry, Stratford-upon-Avon. Stratford is a town dominated by the memory of the achievements of her grandest son, William Shakespeare. His: birthplace; school; wife's parental home (including their courting bench); mother's home; married daughter's home, and final resting place are all on the route travelled by literary pilgrims.

The Bard has left us his final admonition in the church where he is buried:

"Good friend, for Jesus' sake forbear
To dig the dust enclosed here.
Blessed be the man that spares these stones
And cursed be he that moves my bones".

The town itself is a popular tourist attraction with delightful shopping opportunities at the craft, antique and other "folksy" shops. At one of the intimate tea-shops we treated ourselves to home-made cherry pie and ice-cream. Many of the Tudor and Elizabethan houses have been carefully restored and William's birthplace has become a museum in his honour. The much photographed cottage of Will's future wife, Anne Hathaway, lay a few kilometes out of Stratford. He was eighteen years old and she twenty when they married. Until 1911 this lovely thatched house had been home to thirteen generations of Hathaways. We were fortunate to be able to attend and thoroughly enjoy a performance of "Twelfth Night" presented by the Royal Shakespeare Company in their modern theatre on the river Avon. There is another theatre not far away known as "The Other Place". As we were leaving Stratford, I noticed a sticker in the rear window of a parked car which summed it up: "WILL POWER".

The romantic aura surrounding the folk-hero Robin Hood lured us northward to Sherwood Forest, via the city of Nottingham. We took care to avoid the industrial jungles of Birmingham and Coventry en route. At Nottingham we inspected the statues of Robin and his contemporaries: Alan-a-Dale; Will Scarlet; John Little; Friar Tuck and Will Stutely, captured in action poses at the foot of the castle walls (where was Maid Marion?). The castle is 17ᵗʰ century, and very little early Norman architecture remains. As there did not seem to be much else of interest at Nottingham, we moved on to the Forest. Sherwood Forest currently comprises, disappointingly, only scattered fragments of woodland; the original forest had probably been ravaged by the insatiable hunger for charcoal by the Engines of the Industrial Revolution. Fortunately what indigenous forest currently remains appears to be protected. We enjoyed lunch under the trees and afterwards called in at the Visitor's Centre, a small complex of rustic buildings set in a clearing. Here the legend of Robin Hood is creatively displayed in a diorama of the 13ᵗʰ century characters and scenes of the times of "bad" King John's reign.

No specific person has been positively identified as the Robin Hood of the legend, although ancient records hint at a number of possible contenders: a Robyn Hoodes; a Robin Hodes; a nobleman, the Earl of Huntingdon; and another, one Robin from the town of Locksley. Who the historical person may have been is less important than the principles that he is said to have espoused, that have been transmitted down the centuries. The worthy Robin symbolizes that eternal struggle against class injustice, immoderate taxation and bureaucratic excess that bedevils humanity. The villains of the piece were "wicked" King John (who was ultimately humbled by his barons into signing the Magna Carta in 1215, his penultimate year as sovereign) and the Sheriff of Nottingham, the archetypal tax gatherer. There is no evidence however, of direct conflict between Robin Hood and the Norman sheriff of the day. The myth of robbing the rich to feed the poor is in all likelihood simply a romantic folk-tale – although the rich were undoubtedly robbed since there was not much point in robbing the poor. In the Forest, we admired the ancient oak tree known as Major Oak. This tree, to all appearances enjoying robust good health, has a girth of ten metres. As a living link across the centuries, the Major, but for his deficiency in the gift of speech, would have had a fascinating yarn to relate.

We pushed on northwards and at Chesterfield gawped at the church-with-a-crooked–steeple. This oddity, a steeple with a slight banana-shaped curve, has not escaped Man's predilection for Explanations, and theories range from differential shrinkage in the rafters to a notion that it was caused by the devil having alighted on the steeple.

If we were to see anything of Wales, Cornwall and Devon, we could not travel further north. The sand of our time remaining was now accelerating alarmingly through the neck of the travel hour-glass. We had only managed to reach a point about halfway up the British Island and would have to forego the pleasures of Yorkshire and Scotland higher up. Heading westward we stopped at the small market town of Congleton for a browse, and soon after arrived at Chester, an old Roman settlement. Many town names contain the suffix "chester" or "caster", and this identifies their Roman origin, the words cognate with the Latin "castra" meaning "camp". Chester has preserved its architectural heritage in the well-kept condition of its medieval dwellings, and is further blessed with a broad river, the Dee. We experienced the Dee more directly by hiring a small motor-boat and sputtering about in a haze of blue smoke. We later found a grassy campsite at Prestatyn on the Welsh north coast, not far from Chester. This is the land of "Jones", as almost every second business sign declares. Near our site lay a rambling mock-castle that had been built by a "feudal lord" in 1850. There are ramparts, turrets, castellations, loopholes and portcullises, as well, no doubt, as an annual maintenance bill that ensures a regular turn-over of ownership. The current owner, not in residence, was attempting to defray running expenses by staging a flea-market, a jousting tournament and other paying diversions. The joust was well performed with authentic-looking "knights" charging each other in the lists to cries of "Zounds" and "Egad" in a vigorous and entertaining manner. Colourfully emblazoned pennants crackling in the breeze completed the setting.

As we turned south we realized rather painfully that we had, in a sense, reached the "end" of our journeying and were now homeward bound: heading for Amsterdam, and our departure for South Africa. Nevertheless we would seek out whatever diversions we could manage en route. We had been blessed with unusually good weather and our ten year old camper was running like an adolescent, shrugging off the twenty thousand kilometers thus far chalked-up, without complaint. We spent most of the next day driving slowly southward through Wales: passing through shade-dappled, stream-riven, Snowdonia National Park; and then rural countryside – patchwork fields of yellow and orange through gaps in the hedgerows flanking roads barely wide enough to accommodate the camper, and then not always as the undergrowth occasionally brushed our flanks (as I silently prayed for an absence of oncoming traffic). Cows, sheep and stone cottages exuded pastoral pacifism. The names of villages were unpronounceable, and at Aberystwyn we again caught a glimpse of the sea. Stopping at a small village for tea, we visited the local curiosity – a dog's grave. The legend: a squire in the olden days had a faithful and beloved dog that, while the master was away, had come upon a wolf in their cottage. The wolf had killed the squire's two children and the dog immediately set upon the wolf. A fierce battle ensued that ended in the death of the wolf. The badly savaged dog then awaited his master's return. On his arrival at the cottage, and presented with the awful scene, the father of the unfortunate children misread the situation: in his grief–stricken state he assumed his dog was responsible for the death of his children, whereupon he hacked the poor dog to death in a fit of revenge. Having done so, he then noticed the dead body of the wolf and the truth of what had transpired became tragically clear. What else could he do but bury them all? Today it is the dog's courage and loyalty that is remembered.

We stayed the night in Lampeter, in a field whose proprietor had quaintly provided ablution facilities in the form of a stand-pipe and WC at the back of his house. Camping facilities in England and Wales did not always measure up to those on the Continent, but this was usually compensated for by the gentleness of their settings – soft ground, lush grass, open fields in their vicinity (for pre-breakfast rambles) and benign atmosphere.

Our departure from Wales was by a dramatic leap across the River Severn via a modern suspension bridge. Isambard Kingdom Brunel, the innovative 19th century engineer, designed the still-operational rail bridge alongside, and posterity is reminded of this fact by the three metre letters emblazoned on a huge circular steel column: "IKB". We would now follow the coastline as far as possible, and the first stop was at Clovelly, on Bideford Bay. Clovelly is a privately owned fishing village whose houses cling tenaciously to a steep hillside. The place is liberally inhabited by cats and lavishly adorned with banks, even hedges, of fuschias. Luxuriant flower boxes line the steep cobbled walk down to the tiny harbor, altogether producing a delightful effect. We rested awhile on the jetty and soaked up the afternoon ambience: wheeling, complaining seagulls; myriad reflections; painted fishing boats; the lap and gurgle of the sea. On the way out the following day, we called in at the view-site at Hartland Point and found a desolated, rocky promontory guarded by a lighthouse. Evidence of the need for guarding could be seen in the form of a wrecked ship lying broken-backed across an offshore reef. As any shipwreck must do when viewed in calm conditions after the "event", this maritime skeleton evoked a sense of her futile struggle against the power of the sea: was there panic aboard, loss of life? We followed the indented coastline to Tintagel, reputed to have been the home of the Pendragon called Uther, and birthplace of his son, the legendary Arthur, future king. Tintagel castle, built circa 1145, is perched dizzily on a sheer promontory from which there is a magnificent view of the coastline. Nearby lies the town of Camelford where King Arthur's castle, Camelot, was supposed to have been sited.

We now headed inland across Cornwall to intercept the south coast at Looe, another typically charming fishing village. The quay was lined with shops and boys fishing for crabs; and the salty air was alive with the sound of seagulls shrieking irritably overhead. In the shops we found "state of the art" shell-craft: figurines, jewelry, lamps and bric-a-brac. At a pub, The Buller's Arms, we were initiated into the world of "scrumpy", a local alcoholic beverage. We purchased a flagon of the brew for later consumption – the container depicted a broad-horned steer wearing a blissful expression. A slogan bore the promise: "Legless but Smiling".

Now eastward into Devon, we drove through the Dartmoor National Park. This is an expanse of gently rolling hills some six hundred square kilometres in extent. Occasional herds of wild ponies roam freely, but could not be approached closer than about fifty metres. The surrounding landscape comprises large stretches of heather: a blanket of lilac. Roughly in the centre of the Park, on the outskirts of the village of Princetown, lies the notorious

19th century H.M. Dartmoor Prison, which at this time contained about five hundred inmates. Its massive, grey cell blocks squat dully behind a perimeter wall and a sinister absence of sound or movement within creates a feeling of relief by simply being on the outside. We hurried on to dispel these sombre images and stopped at an extremely pretty village with the unlikely name of Lustleigh. Painters and sketchers were at work capturing the spirit of the timbered, thatched cottages set among flowering shrubs and climbing roses. The village sports field must produce interesting and lively matches as the only area of level ground is the cricket pitch.

Carrying on along the coast, we visually sampled the Dorset resorts of Durdle Door and Stairhole with their weird rock formations – the inhospitable temperature of the water prevented our tactile sampling of the sea. Salisbury, also known as New Sarum, lay forty kilometres out of our way to the north, and we felt we could not bypass this historic area. The great Gothic cathedral at Salisbury has the tallest spire in all of England. The impressive interior and spacious grounds afforded us a pleasant hour's exploration. An interesting diversion offered to visitors at many English cathedrals is the opportunity of creating rubbings of brass plaques depicting historical persons, insignia and crests. Melody decided to try one and acquired a sheet of dark paper, a gold-coloured wax crayon and a choice of brasses. By rubbing the crayon over the paper that is held firmly over the brass (which school child has not rubbed coins in this manner?) a presentable copy is produced, right down to the "brass" colour.

Not far from Salisbury, on the Plain, stands an incredible mystery – Stonehenge. Colossal menhirs were brought to this place from Wales (it is thought) some eight millennia ago and erected in concentric circles with huge lintel slabs across the three metre uprights. At a distance, the stones resemble a gathering of cloaked sages in quiet communion: one of their years a century of ours. Remarkable it is to consider that when these very stones were erected; when these very lintels were positioned; man had probably just invented farming, and the use of metals had yet to be discovered. More remarkably, that we have this megalithic monument at all – having been spared the vicissitudes of time and weather and the destructive hand of man. (It is indeed a bitter indictment of our society to observe that a security fence has recently been erected around the stones for their protection). Most remarkably is the fact that men and women of the Druidic tradition still worship at this magical place at certain seasons. To reach the present age of the stone circles, Salisbury cathedral will have to stand until 9500 AD!

Awed, we left this site of ancient mystery and carried on to Winchester, further east. There was good camping at the municipal sports centre, with tree-lined canals and a large duck population. While travelling we generally saved bread scraps in a store known as "the duck bread". This was soon depleted by the voracious ducks at Winchester who seemed to have insatiable appetites. Every time we tossed a few crusts into the water, a scramble of flapping, paddling birds thrashed through the water in a race for the tid-bits. Winchester was the capital of the Anglo-Saxon kingdom at the time of the Norman Conquest and we enjoyed visiting the beautifully restored Great Hall. This is the only vestige of the original medieval castle that was destroyed by Oliver (anti-royalist) Cromwell during the 17th century. We admired King Arthur's Round Table mounted on the west wall – a sturdy oak construction six metres in diameter. The names of Arthur's knights were painted around the circumference and a large figure of the king graces the centre, seated above a Tudor Rose. Although the painted decoration was executed in 1522 for King Henry VIII, the table was first mentioned in the Hall Records of 1360 and even then it was venerated as an object of great age. Winchester the town has a bustling "country village" atmosphere with much space set aside as pedestrian malls. The Norman influence is nowhere more obvious than in the architecture of the cathedral, with its square, squat tower over the intersection of nave and transept. The cathedral's large stained-glass gable window is surely unique. During WWII an explosion caused the original window to collapse. The good folk of the day, with a view to preserving the original glass, re-used the fragments in the replacement of the window in a random, kaleidoscopic fashion. The biblical scenes depicted in the original window are of course no longer discernible, but they are nevertheless there – merely rearranged somewhat. In the cemetery precinct of the cathedral there stands a tombstone bearing the following epitaph:

In Memory of
THOMAS FLETCHER

a Grenadier in the North Reg. of Hants Militia who died of a violent Fever contracted by drinking Small Beer when hot on the 12th of May 1764. Aged 26 Years.

In grateful remembrance of whofe univerfal good will towards his Comrades this Stone is placed here at their expence as a fmall teftimony of their regard and concern.

Here fleeps in peace a Hampfhire Grenadier.
Who caught his death drinking cold fmall beer.
Soldiers be wise from his untimely fall
And when ye're hot drink Strong or none at all.

This memorial being decay'd was reftor'd by the Officers of the Garrifon A.D. 1781

An honeft Soldier never is forgot
Whether he die by Mufket or by Pot.

Our next stop and final campsite in England was at Brighton, where Mark would leave us to return to London for a further sixteen months. Brighton is the popular holiday resort noted for its two piers: the old and the new, and more recently a modern yacht marina. The new pier (the old one has been closed down) contains amusement arcades in deliciously bad taste. Peggy and I invested 10p each in the pursuit of New Experience, in the form of a helter-skelter ride. Armed with small coir mats, we climbed the wooden staircase and then launched ourselves down the helical channel, emerging much like newspaper bales from the printers. Back on the beach we were pleasantly surprised that the traditional Punch and Judy puppet show is still alive. Punch is still the classical wife-beater who, for what appeared to be a miniscule provocation, would violently thrash poor Judy with a long stick. This traditional violence, as portrayed in this mini-tableau of Life between the Sexes, possibly symbolizes the violent trend of modern films that mostly perpetuate Punch's anti-social behavior, the long stick having been replaced by the longer stick of a firearm. Oddly the small crowd of children watching the performance did not respond as enthusiastically as expected at the perennial repartee between puppets and audience when Punch proclaims: "Oh yes he did!" and children would shout: "Oh no he didn't!", and there was not the usual urgency to warn Punch that there was a crocodile creeping up behind him. In the face of such diversions as video, films, and electronic games it is perhaps surprising that Punch and Co. survive at all. I suspect their future will be short. An unexpected sight for us was the candy-coloured, oriental-style building with onion domes and spires: the summer palace of King George IV, about a hundred years old.

With the day of departure back to South Africa now only a week away, the fleeting hours seemed all the more precious. We headed for Dover along the coastal road from where we had occasional glimpses of France. In Hastings we stopped for a while to watch a cricket match, played in genteel English fashion. All the ingredients were there: shade trees on the boundary; the somnolent hum of a summer afternoon; the characteristic crack of leather on willow; the muffled voices of the players changing fielding positions as overs ended; polite clapping from spectators if something happened on the field. A fellow spectator was a member of the local constabulary enjoying the match from his squad car. Hastings was clearly not a crime-ravaged town. By late afternoon we had reserved a berth on the Dover-Calais midnight special.

With the evening before us, we felt that our last evening in England should be celebrated by dining out. Dover did not offer much by way of diversion so we drove to nearby Folkstone. A ramble through the quaint old-quarter acquainted us with what fare was available in the restaurants. One window advertised six or seven dishes, and each had the appendage "+ chips". This included "cottage-pie + chips" and "curry and rice + chips". We chose another restaurant. We ordered "Shepherd's pie and vegetables", our unanimous selection (sans chips), and we awaited developments. Eventually our repast arrived and we were immediately struck by the similarity between our dinners and something we had seen somewhere… sometime… Was it Mont St. Michel at high tide? The shepherd's pie was an island in a bright green sea of pea-water that, apart from the aesthetic shock it produced, had the effect of severely contaminating the taste of the island-pie. As dinner it was more a gastronomic counterfeit. A measure of consolation was salvaged from the evening (misery loves company) by the sorrowful entertainment provided by a fellow diner. This poor fellow had sent his plate back to the kitchen three or four times, the management not able to comprehend or correct the deficiency. His dinner partner stabbed listlessly at her food, momentarily brightening each time his plate returned from the kitchen in the hope of having a participating dinner companion.

BACK TO FRANCE AND
BACK TO HOLLAND

A midnight ferry journey, and before we knew it, we were driving on French soil. I was by this time beginning to "go vague" as to which side of the road to be driving on. We crept into a small field near Dunkirk to sleep away the few remaining hours of the night, and in the morning drove to the beach. The blustery, overcast day complemented the conjuring up images of one of the more dramatic and poignant military withdrawals in the history of warfare. When the Nazi fist had punched the British Expeditionary Force back to the beach at Dunkirk during June 1940, it became a vital matter for England to evacuate her hundreds of thousands of troops without delay. The Royal Navy ferried 13 000, 20 000 and 45 000 in the first three nights of the operation when the Admiralty made a call for public assistance. Responding, between five hundred and eight hundred private craft of all shapes and sizes, swarmed across the Channel without thought of thanks or reward in a stirring example of courage and devotion. The men were safely returned to England and potential disaster averted. Grains of sand tumbled along the wide, flat beach; threads of spume flitted across the small breakers; a gull cried – and the spell was broken.

The land is flat and featureless along the north coast of France and Belgium and by late afternoon we had entered the Netherlands, our final country. We were assailed by bitter-sweet memories – the picturesque houses with their window displays of growing things, carefully revealed to passersby by the parted lace curtains; dykes, canals, cyclists and lush meadows – the country that, in short, provided us with our initial European impressions in that crisp freshness of March, six month earlier. We found an excellent campsite for the night at Den Haag.

The next day saw the final leg of our trip when we reached Amsterdam, our original point of arrival, now our point of departure. We had come full "circle", the perimeter of which measured 20 000 kilometres. We camped at the delightful Amsterdamse Bos for the last time while arrangements were made to find a buyer for the campervan, and to take stock of the souvenirs and mementos assiduously gathered over the months. We optimistically bought two large, cheap, cardboard suitcases to accommodate the extras that we had accumulated. We had four days in hand and we used them to explore this city of 100 canals and 1000 bridges, initially by guided tour-boat. We passed a Cats' Home, situated on a house-boat, the "inmates" in various attitudes of indolent repose on the deck; a view of the narrowest house in Amsterdam, 1,8 metres in width, barely perceptible between the typical four storey high-gabled houses flanking it. Most houses have a beam projecting from the gable high above the roadway, its function to lift and negotiate furniture through window openings that cannot be carried up the narrow staircases within. Amsterdam seen from the canals was a rewarding experience, as one picturesque scene followed another, often framed by an arched or tilt-up bridge. Back ashore our hearing was assaulted by an English "punk" group in an impromptu pavement concert on the square known as the Damrak, as well as several bugle bands in the vicinity – a cacophony of sound.

We window-shopped through the Zeedijk, an area of ill repute, and were intrigued by the merchandise on display. Scantily clad ladies were comfortably seated behind shop-fronts, backlit with a reddish glow, in the hopes of attracting a customer. One such, a rather buxom wench, had fallen asleep at her post and was teetering precariously on the edge of her stool. Was this a case of overwork or underwork? I lingered in the hope of witnessing the outcome of this incipient instability, but was unceremoniously dragged off by Peggy.

From the ridiculous to the sublime: we paid a visit to the Rijksmuseum Art Gallery where a high point was Rembrandt's "Nightwatch", a work that fairly leaps out of its frame with its creative dynamism. Fascinating were the exhibits in the modern art section: the metre high metal sculpture of a skeletal human figure with a small radio fitted into its head, the speaker, appropriately, the mouth. An arm was linked to the tuner and operated by a motor-driven, eccentric crank that rocked the tuner back and forth across a pre-selected station on the radio, resulting in a rhythmical interchange of unintelligible sound and silence. Quite bizarre. There were folded surfaces cleverly painted to produce a startling kinetic effect as one passed by. Or the montage of thousands of unused postage stamps of various denominations arranged in an artistic blend of shadings. Many paintings, sketches (e.g. "curtain across a valley"), collages, and sculptures appeared to be "meaningless", but yet stimulated the un-plumbed depths of one's emotional psyche. I guess.

One outstanding work, entitled "The Beanery", was a full-scale replica of an American restaurant/bar through which the viewer was permitted to wander. We mingled with the dummy "patrons" lining the bar counter and sitting at tables. The "bar-tender" stands behind a counter polishing a glass; a mirrored wall behind him reflects rows of (fake) alcoholic beverages; a silent juke-box stands in the corner: altogether a tableau frozen in time, completely true to life. Except for one detail that transforms an otherwise ordinary scene into something so weird that it feels uncomfortable: where each "person's" face should normally be, the artist had substituted the face of a clock!

A pleasant stroll along a boulevard brought us to the Van Gogh Museum. This man created prodigiously – drawings, paintings, sketches - by the hundred. There was the Kroller-Muller Museum at Arnhem devoted to his works; here was another. In most major galleries his work will be found and of course there are many more in private hands. To say we enjoyed Vincent's genius would sound rather trite, nevertheless we found much satisfaction during our short stay in the museum. Outside, set apart in a small space, we found a strange and poignant memorial. Tall stainless-steel plates were arranged in a spiral convolution of diminishing height. In a regular rhythm of ascending and descending tones, a deep, but soft, throbbing sound could be heard. A plaque advised that here was a memorial to the women who had died in the concentration camps of WWII.

The following day we sold the camper. It was quite a wrench, having served us so faithfully as home and transport for six months, and the ladies' eyes were more than a little moist.

D-Day! 2 September 1983. Our flight back to Johannesburg was due to depart at 15:15 hours. "D" for depths of desperate depression as the carefree gypsy life was to be snuffed out? Or "D" for dogged determination to defy domesticity and begin saving for the next trip? Time, in its usual supercilious manner, would tell. In the meantime an awesome array of baggage lay spread across the campsite lawn. Our collection of stones, shells, potsherds and other unclassifiable junk were crammed into the suitcases and the camp supervisor arranged for a taxi to convey us to Schipol Airport.

It required a great effort of will to ensure the taxi-driver's co-operation when he arrived to find: 3 travellers; 3 backpacks; 3 bulging airline bags; 1 briefcase swollen with maps and travel brochures; 2 large cardboard suitcases; 1 unwieldly bundle comprising: 2 folding chairs, 3 camp stools and 1 folding table, all sturdily lashed together, not to mention assorted personal hand- and shoulder-bags (what on earth was I thinking?). The driver was distinctly heard to mumble that had he known this was waiting for him, he would never have responded to the call. However, he probably took comfort in the fact that the airport was only a five minute drive away and he coped manfully, notwithstanding the various sharp objects poking him in the ribs.

At the airport, cruel fate had a last-minute joke in store for us. Upon arrival at the airport building, I nonchalantly checked in our luggage. The second mistake I made was in sending the suitcases containing our least valuable goods (in other words, the junk) into the maw of the airport receiving system before the backpacks and other more important bags. My first mistake had been to overlook the wise precaution of initially pre-weighing our total cargo, which would have avoided the trauma that followed. As it happened, the final tally of our luggage weight was duly calculated. I came close to cardiac arrest when told that collectively, we were 50 kilograms over our free baggage allowance. This did not even include the pathetic little bundle of camp furniture. Translated into meaningful terms, this represented a sum to be paid of 2500 Dutch guilders, about R 1 000! Desperately affixing an expression of abject misery at this news, I was granted the concession of being surcharged only 10 kg provided that one of the large suitcases was discarded. The surcharge amounted to R 200, a princely sum to pay for Greek stones, bottles and clay fragments of indeterminable antiquity that would never serve as pots again. Still, this was the best that the abject expression could manage, and we moved into phase 2 of fate's little joke. Naturally, the two large suitcases, one of which was to be sacrificed, had by this time disappeared on the conveyor belt. The pieces of the nightmare were beginning to mesh nicely. At least we had about an hour to take action. Peggy and I were allowed to descend into the bowels of the freight section, under the close surveillance of a strapping Dutch security lady. Once we had located the suitcases, the task began of clearing out of one of them of the most dispensable articles to make room for the least dispensable articles emerging from the other suitcase.

A strange scene was thus being enacted in the bowels of the terminal amidst the loading operations busily dispatching freight to the dozen or more international airliners waiting on the apron above. Setting to, I worked myself into a lather of sweat at the outset in merely untying the ropes around the suitcases which I had stoutly tied not long before in anticipation of the vigorous treatment they were bound to receive from luggage handlers. The tying had in any case become necessary as a result of the fabric of the suitcases manifesting incipient disintegration having received a light sprinkling of rain the night before. The lids were eventually thrown open to reveal the mélange of a wide variety of hastily packed articles. As the contents were disgorged for sorting, the area began to look like the preparations for setting up a pavement stall at Portobello Road flea-market. Our lady custodian almost managed to suppress a wave of mirth from rippling across her countenance while maintaining a stern look of patient authority. With an eye on the clock, Peggy and I now fiercely tackled the contents: Wellington boots were ripped out, an archery arrow laid to one side, semi-crumpled aluminium pots (the storm at Mont St.Michel swam before my eyes) were unceremoniously cast aside along with crockery, cutlery, pine cones from the Black Forest, Greek pebbles, shoes, towels, the number and variety of articles emerging seemed without end. Eventually the sacrificial suitcase, camp furniture as well as gas cooker, lamp and spare gas canister (the airline refused this anyway), were handed over to an astonished attendant in the "left luggage" section, to do with as his discretion, or business acumen, dictated.

Life returned to normal and we had just enough time remaining to visit the airport shops to do the gift-shopping for family and friends back home – inevitably left till the last moment.

We boarded the airliner for the overnight flight with stops, again, at Frankfurt and Ilha de Sol, and settled into our seats with heads well stocked with impressions and memories of a fabulous experience.

END

APPENDICES

Appendix I : Tips from Peggy on things domestic.

Appendix II : Practical hints on Documentation, Baggage and Transportation.

Appendix III : Ten Commandments for Travelers and a Warning.

APPENDIX I

Tips from Peggy on things domestic

It is said that cleanliness is next to Godliness. Forget all about that. Godliness you get more than enough of, what with visits to untold cathedrals and awe-inspiring walks through magnificent natural forests opening out on vistas of towering, snow-clad peaks. Cleanliness of body is easily come by as every campsite boasts showers with water in varying degrees of hot. One campsite in Italy (Pompeii) even had a most welcome bathtub. Cleanliness of clothing is altogether another story. Germany, Holland and Switzerland, among the more technological countries, had campsites that had at least one fully automatic washing machine accompanied by a drier (coin operated). There was usually a queue! Get used to washing clothes in cold water in most other countries and do not forget a wash-line. Clothes pegs are absolutely invaluable for all sorts of things. Avoid my mistake and purchase three or four pairs of BLACK boxer shorts for husband/boy-friend before leaving home. I had bought white ones and cursed washdays for it. The plastic carrier-bags that are supplied by our supermarkets are almost unknown in Europe and if you can find them you have to pay for them. So don't forget to take at least a dozen – they do not take up much room. They are very handy for storing dirty washing, shopping, as rubbish bins, etc. and are also useful for packing damp washing en route to the next campsite.

Now, for the "inner man". France wins hands down on supermarkets! Their "hyper" shops really do stock everything under one roof, and they make ours look like corner grocery stores. We ladies were fascinated and it always took an effort of will to leave the store. We were astounded to see in Italy the vast array of pastas of all shapes and sizes, undreamed of by us "peasants" who know only of spaghetti and macaroni. The fruit and vegetables in supermarkets were magnificent – so fresh, and what a range of exotic fruit. Mango-steens, kiwi-fruit, avocadoes, etc. It was rather difficult to decipher the contents of tins and packages that did not have a picture printed on the label. Meat was very expensive in most countries and we were surprised to see how little meat was on display. Germany specialized in smoked meats and sausages and very delicious they were, although expensive. We dined mostly on tinned fish or vegetable dishes, usually on a staple such as rice, pasta and, once we had discovered it in France, cous-cous, a type of Algerian grain only needing boiling water poured over it to prepare. German bread, especially the heavy brown variety, took a bit of getting used to – I'm sure you could use this bread as building blocks. We generally purchased our bread from little bakeries that wafted the most delectable aromas of newly baked bread. This bread went stale in a very short time, however, and usually ended up in the plastic bag labeled "duck-bread". On occasion we arrived at our destination after the bakeries had closed and gratefully hauled out the "duck-bread". We were astonished to find tins of KOO jam in Germany, the cheapest on the shelves. We laid in good stocks of this as jams were otherwise fairly expensive. In Greece we lived almost exclusively on their legendary yoghurt and honey. Foodstuffs here were embarrassingly cheap and one fondly remembers such "perks" as roadside stalls selling tomatoes at 5 kg for 20 cents. We thought the Greeks baked the finest bread in Europe. The sea-foods and salads were equally outstanding, not to mention the olives and feta (cheese). We acquired a distinct taste for food drenched in olive-oil, the norm in Greece.

All in all, providing meals for ravenous travelers is economically achieved by shopping where the locals are seen to do their shopping and avoiding prepared foods wherever possible. We did not have a fridge, but managed to keep perishables for short periods in a polystyrene cold-box by means of freezable briquettes that we froze in campsite freezers. (Sometimes one is expected to pay for this service).

Two key words describe attributes that help ease the lot of a poor house-wife (camper-wife?), viz: adapt and improvise.

Also, a (relatively) well-fed family is a (relatively) contented family.

APPENDIX II

Practical hints on Documentation, Baggage and Transportation

Documents:

Visas. Obtain these timeously but not too early – some begin "running" from date of issue as opposed to date of entry. They should be valid for "multiple entries" to avoid travel limitations imposed by a "single entry" visa. Be clear as to the expiry date of the visa: from date of issue? or from date of first entry? Do not rely on obtaining visas while overseas, this could be a frustrating and time-consuming exercise.

Passports. It is stating the obvious but ensure that the validity extends well beyond the intended return date. Along with airline ticket, a passport is probably the most important document in your possession. Keep, separately, a certified copy. The passport is scrutinized with relish by border police and sundry bureaucrats who appear to deem the passport of greater worth than the individual bearing it. It may not be going too far to say that to Officialdom a passport is the individual – the accompanying body merely its means of conveyance. Therefore guard the passport! When registering at campsites the passport is invariably requested to be deposited with management as security. This should be resisted. To voluntarily place one's proof of identity and traveler bona fides in the hands of a stranger for possible loss by fire, theft or mismanagement does not make sense. There is an alternative – see next section.

Camping Carnet: an ideal (and often acceptable) substitute for a passport when requested by camp managers as security. It is basically a signed undertaking to respect the Rules of Good Camping and is obtainable from the Automobile Association, as is your:

International Driver's Licence. In a bureaucratic "masterstroke" not all European countries subscribe to the International Convention for driving licences. It will be necessary to obtain the necessary IDL applicable for the intended countries. A few spare passport-size photographs could be useful.

Maps. Apart from a good set of road maps to as large a scale as may be conveniently carried, a vital reference book with an up to date list of the location of campsites is a must. A good directory will not only state the telephone number and describe the facilities of campgrounds in alphabetical sequence, but will in addition indicate their geographical position on thumb-nail maps of the region. This is extremely useful in finding a safe spot to bed down from where you happen to be. A campervan is a land-yacht to be navigated by means of reliable map information, including available campsite "land-falls".

Foreign Language Phrasebooks. While it is obviously not possible to gain a working knowledge of the many European languages likely to be encountered – indeed quite unnecessary due to a widespread understanding of English on the Continent – it is nevertheless useful to know certain foreign words and phrases. Key words would concern foodstuffs: bread, milk, water (potable?); directions: right, left, straight ahead, where is…,? how far….?, campsite? ("campings" is universally understood); numbers: in relation to money values (here too the universality of written numerals can avoid misunderstandings - keep pen and paper handy); public relations: good morning, - day, - evening; please, thank you, good-bye. An attempt to speak in the local tongue is usually appreciated but, beware of using rehearsed and polished sentences – you will be taken for a native speaker and the fluent reply will prove incomprehensible.

Currency. Travellers cheques are a safe form of exchange. It is an advantage to purchase cheques in the currency of regions being visited to avoid commissions when encashing. (Credit cards, and cell phones, were unknown in 1983).

Travel research. There are two opportunities for research: pre and post departure. In either case the purpose of research is to become aware of the possibilities awaiting you concerning a) "people interests" and b) "place interests".

a) People: Entertainments, festivals, carnivals, exhibitions and similar special occasions which are collectively known as "calendar events". These happenings are dynamic, people oriented and are specific to time and place. Sad it would be to pass within a few kilometers of some small village just then celebrating a festival of flowers, folk-dancing, etc. simply through ignorance of the event.

b) Places: Those places and objects of interest that are essentially static and merely require seeking out. Included are galleries, permanent exhibitions, museums, etc. as well as natural wonders such as waterfalls, gorges, caves and coves. Historical places like battlefields, archeological diggings must be researched if the significance of our predecessors' experiences and way of life is to be enlivened and appreciated. This type of research is often best done "in situ" where residual influences may be felt.

Notwithstanding the relevance of research and pre-planning, there is always much pleasure and satisfaction to be derived from a spontaneous and unexpected discovery of something or somewhere strange or unusual. This is possibly the biggest single factor contributing to the sparkle in the Gypsy/ Traveling Life – a new picture round every corner, a sight never seen before and in most cases never to be seen again. Travel literature has a place but beware information overload – careful sifting is necessary. An important source of information from travel brochures is often obtained from tourist bureaux at airports, rail and bus stations and city centres also containing city map, current attractions and campsites.

<u>Baggage</u>. There is an almost universal trend amongst inexperienced travelers to over-estimate their clothing requirements. A few garments easy to wash and quick to dry is preferable to an extensive "wardrobe" which results in heavier suitcases, a bigger "wash", long drying time and often results in a bundle of damp clothing having to be carted about. Common sense items would include good walking shoes, wet and cold weather gear, including gloves. Basic medications and a compact first-aid kit are essential and a pocket calculator for currency conversions is a good idea. Hardly anyone travels without a camera and it is easy to fall into the trap of trying to record "everything". Experience the moment, capturing it is secondary. A photograph will never "feel" the ambience.

<u>Transportation.</u> The most common ways of touring are: a) own transport, either bought or hired; b) public transport, train or coach; c) other people's transport i.e. hitch-hiking; d) the organized tour.

a) Own transport. This offers complete freedom of choice as to routes and timetables. It opens innumerable opportunities for exploration "off the beaten track" and this is no small advantage. The cost of hiring versus buying may be easily assessed by setting off the hire charges against the net cost of the vehicle (purchase price less resale price) over the period of the trip. The resale figure could be assumed to be about 50% of the initial price provided the vehicle is properly maintained, especially the bodywork. As a rule of thumb, purchasing will be more economical if the period exceeds a month. In our case, the net cost of purchasing was about 25% of the cost of hiring over the six month period. There are dealers that offer a "buy back" scheme.

b) Public transport. Here again there is freedom of choice of destination but with several constraints: difficult to do excursions off the main route; difficult to find a campsite near the train/coach terminus.

c) Hitch-hiking. As this method of roving usually appeals to the young and impecunious who will not be reading this, no more will be said. It is not recommended.

d) Organized tours. These are a means of moving, feeding and exposing to travel "sights" a given number of people at any one time. Such folk are spared the inconvenience of arranging and maintaining a travel itinerary, problems associated with feeding, watering and sleeping and all the bureaucratic formalities that bedevil mankind in general and the traveler in particular. There are tours to cater for different age groups and travel tastes, and often appeal to those who have only a few weeks to spare. The organized tour however, has a major drawback. It could be described as "micro future-shock". The swift pace of travelling, seldom in one place for longer than a day or two, an itinerary definitely "on the beaten track", can leave folk weary and confused. We witnessed on occasions sad cases of the "glazed-eye" syndrome among tour group members, especially stragglers, as they formed a human wake in the stern of their tour leader, furled umbrella or magazine held aloft like an ensign. Where several tour groups are active in some place of importance there must exist a real risk of becoming detached from your group, and worse, joining a strange group in error (like an organic compound trading its molecules). There are of course camping tours offered, thus combining economy with the delights of the outdoor life. This is not restricted to the young only. On several occasions in campgrounds we encountered "Das Rollende Hotel", a touring sleeper coach that catered for the not so young, allowing them to camp in comfort in their mobile "home".

Clearly all forms of travelling will remain valid because of the various natures, tastes and circumstances of individuals. There is, I think, a common bond among travelers whether enjoying an extravagant vacation or travelling on a "shoe-string". It is the commonality of mind-broadening experiences, new and unfamiliar vistas and the opportunity to savour an exciting way of life made possible by the temporary release from the grip of daily routine.

APPENDIX III

Ten Commandments for travelers (with acknowledgement to an unknown wit) and a Warning!

THE TEN COMMANDMENTS.

1. Thou shalt not take things too seriously, for a carefree mind is the beginning of a fine holiday.

2. Thou must at all times know where thy passport lies, for a man without a passport is a man without a country.

3. Remember to take half the clothes thou needest and twice the money.

4. Thou shalt not expect to find things as they are at home for thou hath left home to find things different.

5. Thou shalt not worry, for he that worries hath no pleasure. Few things are fatal.

6. Thou shalt not let other tourists get on thy nerves for thou art paying good money to enjoy thyself.

7. When in Rome thou shalt be prepared to do as the Romans do.

8. Thou shalt not judge the entire people of a country by one person who hath given trouble.

9. Remember thou art a guest in other lands and he that treateth his host with respect shall in turn be respected.

10. Thou shouldst remember that if thou were expected to stay in one place, thou would have been created with roots.

WARNING

The bite of the "travel-bug" (feriae amant) is extremely dangerous. This bug has not been positively isolated but it appears that the soles of the feet are vulnerable. An early symptom is the "itchy-feet" that appears to only find relief away from the sufferer's habitual environment. Once infected the disease spreads rapidly through the patient's Way of Life, and his complacency with the existing order is steadily undermined. As the disease becomes established victims react adversely to Routine and Habit. Chronic cases find themselves unable to regard the same surroundings for longer than several days, without breaking out into a rash of restlessness and suffering an impulsive urge to "move on".

Precautions against contracting the disease comprise the following:

a) Avoid travel brochures, books, films and other public media presentation of travel;

b) Avert eyes when passing travel agents' offices and especially avoid looking at large full-colour posters of far-away places. Remember what one glance did for Lot's wife.

c) Shun company that discusses recent or forthcoming trips/tours.

d) Cultivate a belief that the entire world is comprised by one's daily routine and accept that, like the "flat-earthers" nothing really exists beyond the horizon; alternatively if something does exists "out there", it is not worth the trouble knowing about.

e) Protect following generations by eliminating studies such as Geography and History.

f) Consider the following utterance of Socrates to be heretical: "I am a citizen of the world".

g) Despise travelling as time and money wasting, trivial and boring.

There is no known cure for this disease:

YOU HAVE BEEN WARNED!!

BON VOYAGE

Printed in Great Britain
by Amazon